RMarsh

IMPROVISED RESCUE TECHNIQUES

BILL MARCH.

FOREWORD

This little book of diagrams and explanatory notes was written to help candidates for the M.I.C. It will prove invaluable to them, since it fills a very obvious gap in the available literature on Mountain Rescue techniques. In recent years cliff rescue has become almost the sole preserve of the official Mountain Rescue teams, but immediate action must be taken by the climbers themselves, many of whom are woefully ignorant of what they can do in an emergency, with the sort of equipment normally carried. Bill March, deputy Principal at Glenmore Lodge, is one of the very few people qualified to review existing practices. An accomplished climber himself, he is centrally involved with the training and grading of instructors. This experience, coupled with his gifts as a draftsman, has resulted in this valuable booklet. It should be read, not only by those training to be instructors, but by all climbers.

ERIC LANGMUIR.

C O N T E N T S

List of Illustrations

INTRODUCTION

This book is not intended to be a fully comprehensive work on self rescue technique but rather a synthesis of basic techniques. There are many different solutions to problems of rescue and I have attempted to show one or two methods which may be used. The important point is to practice the techniques in controlled situations when all the normal mistakes can be made in safety. It will be found that points such as the length of sling and position of karabiner are critical and these should be determined by experience and practice.

BILL MARCH.

CHAPTER I.

ROPE, KNOTS AND HARNESSES.

CHAPTER I.

ROPE, KNOTS AND HARNESS.

The rope is the minimum basic equipment carried by the mountaineer, and in a rescue situation it is his most important aid. The rope carried depends upon the type of activity; a party leader in charge of a group of hill walkers will carry a 120 ft. of No.2 or 7mm nylon rope, and a rock climber 120 ft. of No.4 or 11mm nylon rope, or 300 ft. No.3 or 9mm rope depending upon the standard of the route. The rope itself may be of two types: hawser laid with three strands of nylon filaments twisted in a spiral, and kernmantel where the fibres are arranged longitudinally in the core and the whole covered with a "braided sheath" There is little to choose between the strength and elasticity of the two types of rope in a rescue situation. The kernmantel rope is more resistant to abrasion, easier to handle and less liable to kink than the spiral laid rope. The hawser laid rope has the advantage that the three strands can be unravelled and joined together in an emergency, thus increasing the rope length by three, and of course decreasing its strength proportionately.

BASIC KNOTS

Figure of 8

This is usually tied on a loop of rope and used as the end tie on climbing. It is a strong knot adjusted by feeding one strand of the rope through the knot and tightening afterwards. Its great advantage is it is comparatively easy to tie and if tied wrongly, is still quite safe as an overhand knot, or as an expanded figure of 8. The end tail of rope should be tied off in a thumb knot around the main rope.

Bowline

This is the old classic knot in climbing which is not as strong as the figure of eight knot but still in common use as a direct tie onto the rope. Easily adjusted by feeding through on one side of the knot. This knot is not always effective in kernmantel rope and should always be tied off with a thumb knot around the main rope.

Sheet Bend

A useful knot used for joining rope of unequal thickness and for joining slings which need to be adjusted easily. May be tied single or double and also can be locked with a thumb knot.

Fisherman Knot

Used for joining two ropes together. Can be tied single or double.

Tape Knot

The only knot to use for fastening tape slings.

BASIC KNOTS

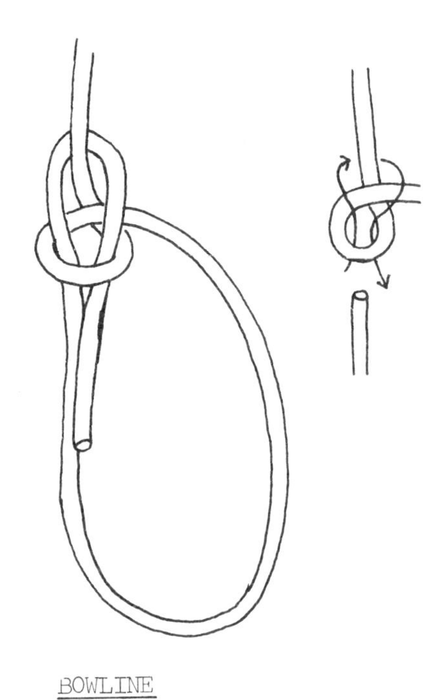

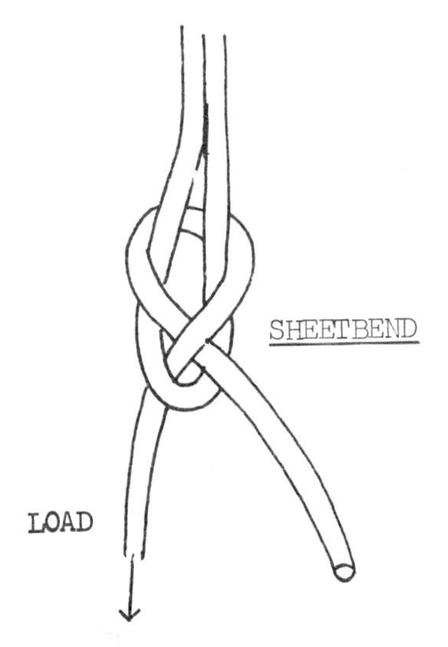

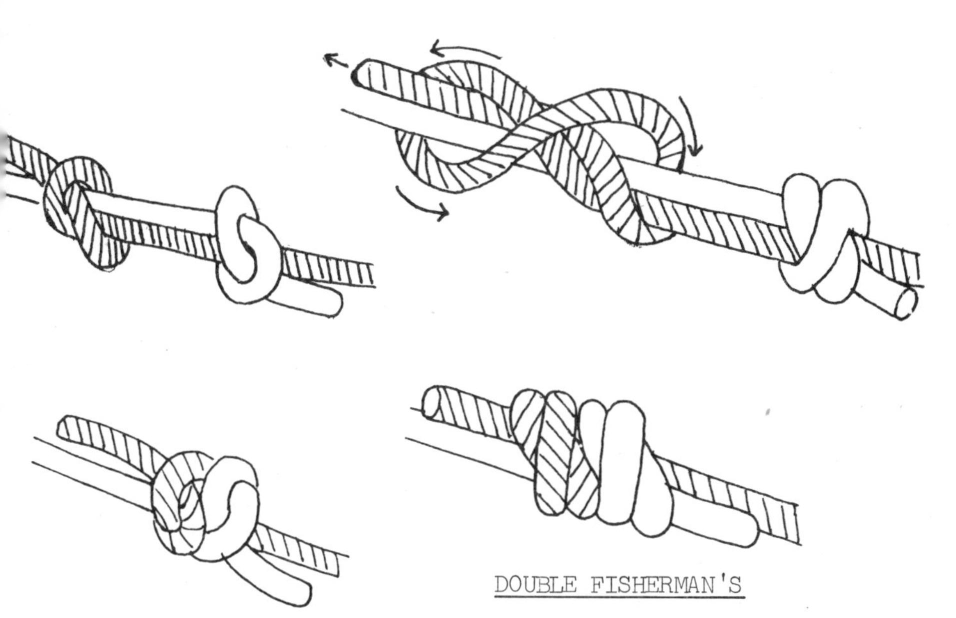

DOUBLE FISHERMAN'S

SINGLE FISHERMAN'S

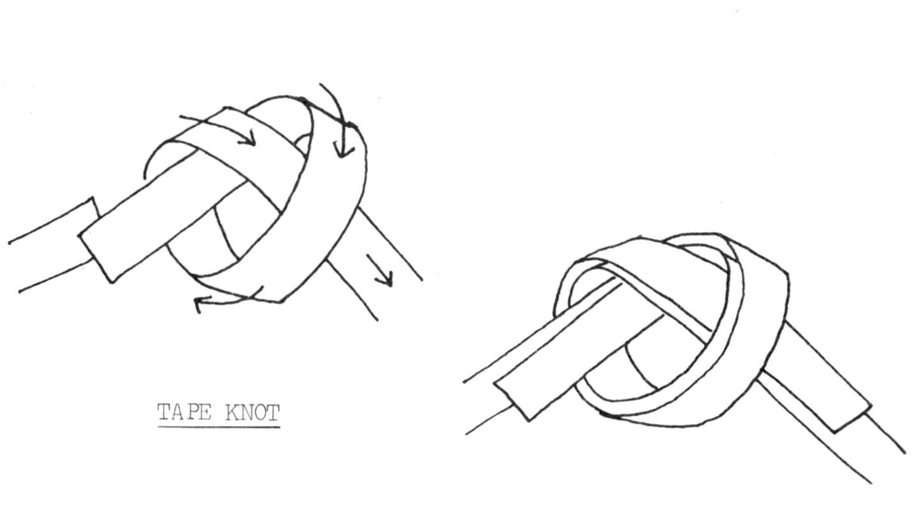

TAPE KNOT

Bowline on the Bight

This is simply a bowline tied on a bight of rope with the end loop passed over the half completed knot (see diagram). It gives an easily adjusted sit sling with two loops for the legs, or may be used as a shoulder harness with a loop crossed over each shoulder and under the opposite arm. The harness can be tightened by feeding one strand of rope through the knot.

Figure of Eight on the Bight

This is a single figure of eight knot tied on a bight of rope with the end loop passed over the completed knot. (see diagram). It is used in the same way as the Bowline on the bight.

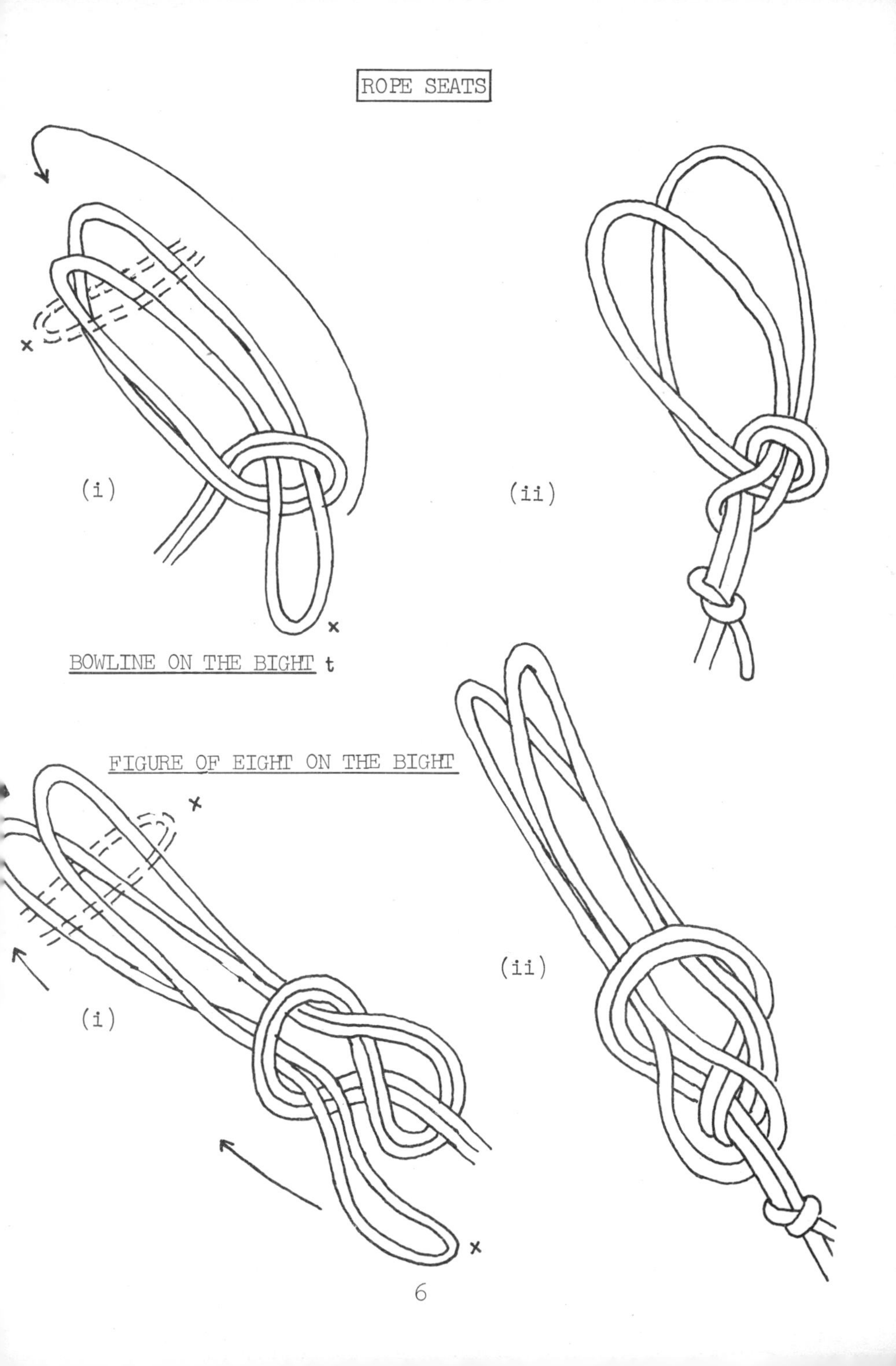
ROPE SEATS
x
(i)
x
(ii)
BOWLINE ON THE BIGHT t
FIGURE OF EIGHT ON THE BIGHT
x
(i)
(ii)
x

Triple Bowline

The triple bowline is a bowline tied in a bight of rope and gives three loops which can be worn as a sit sling, chest sling, or a full harness. All harnesses are tightened up by feeding one strand of rope right through the knot and the harness. This takes some time but it is essential that the harness is a secure fit on the body.

(a) Sit sling - one loop around the chest and one for each leg.

(b) Chest harness - one loop under the arm pits and around the chest, the other two crossed over the shoulder and under the arm pits.

(c) Full harness - one loop for each leg and one diagonally across one shoulder and under the opposite arm pit. The harness is adjusted so that the knot is above the centre of gravity - just below the sternum. The loops at the back may all be clipped together with a karabiner or tied together with a sling to give greater security.

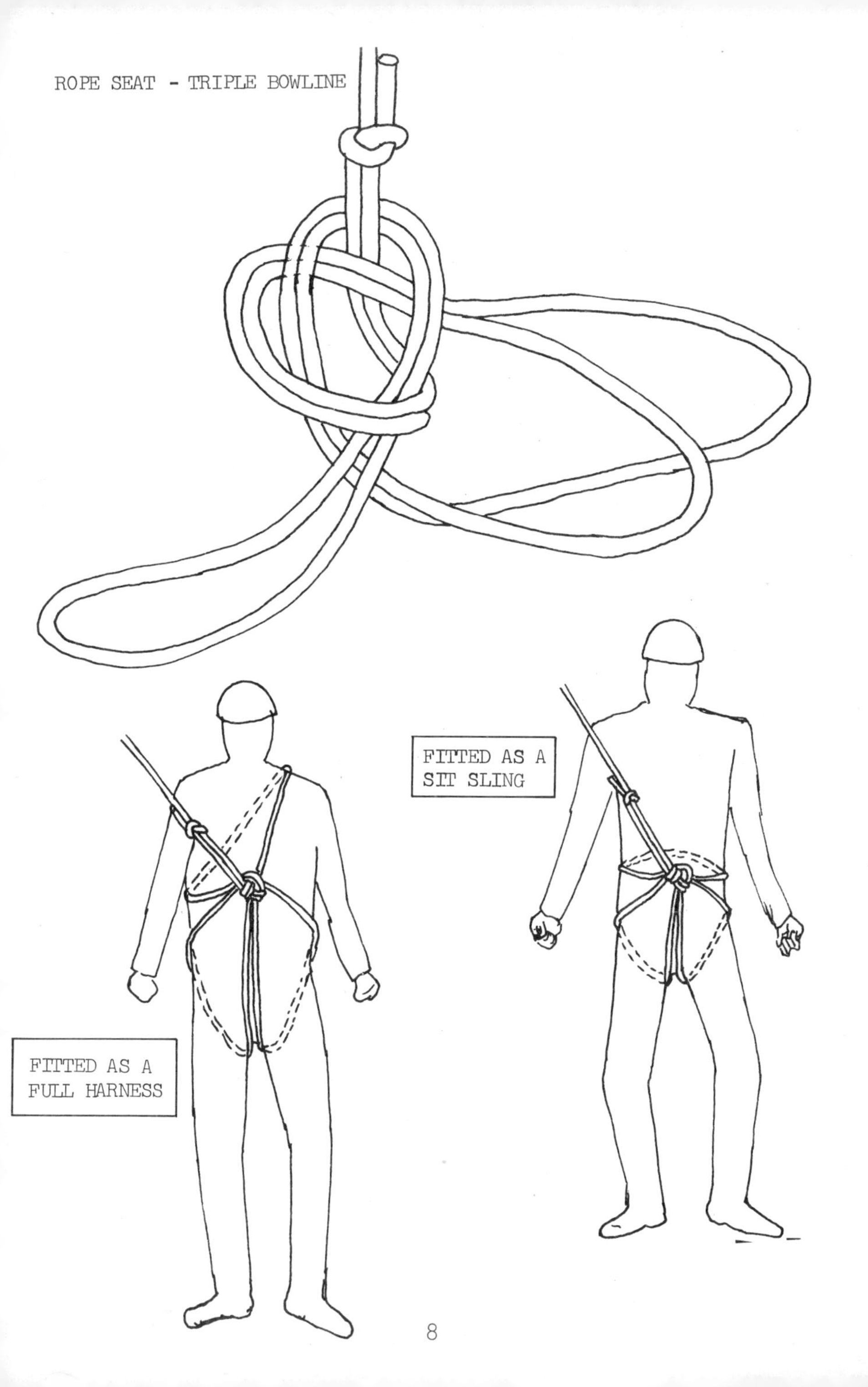
ROPE SEAT - TRIPLE BOWLINE
FITTED AS A
SIT SLING
FITTED AS A
FULL HARNESS

Sit Slings

Slings are a standard piece of equipment carried by climbers. Some should be of the required length to be used for making improvised sit slings and chest harnesses. One inch tape slings make very comfortable harnesses which are less cumbersome than the rope slings.

Dulfer Seat

This is one of the most comfortable sling seats and is easily arranged. Take a sling and karabiner and pass around the back at waist level. Drop one loop of the sling weighted with a karabiner at back and pull through the legs. Clip onto the two loops of the sling held in the front. This gives support to the waist and both legs. The karabiner can be clipped into the waistline to hold the seat up.

Double Sit Sling Seat

Step into a doubled sling crossed at the front, drop one loop at the back and pull up between the legs to clip onto the front with a karabiner.

Figure of Eight Seat

Twist a sling to form a figure of eight and step into the two loops. Clip a karabiner at the cross over point and up into the waistline. If the sling is too long, tie off the surplus in an overhand knot to get the required tension.

Thigh Loop

A quick sit sling is a short loop around the thigh clipped into the waistline.

SIT SLINGS

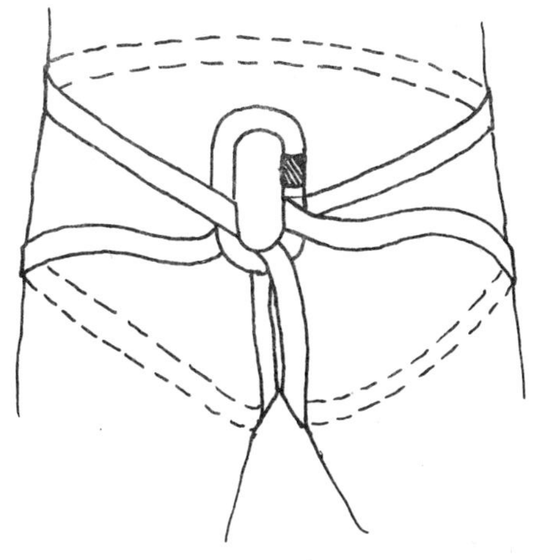

DULFER SEAT

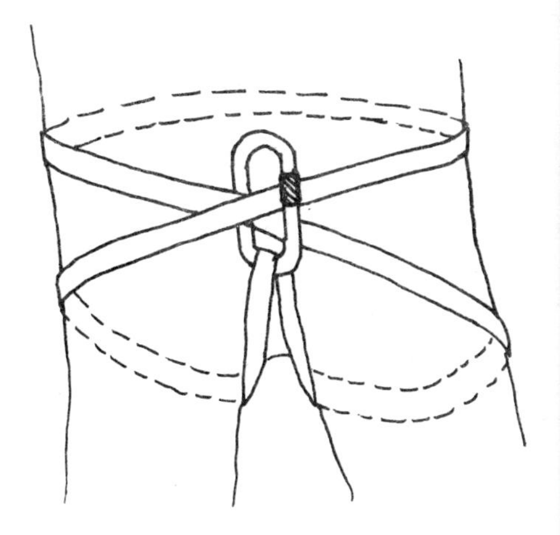

DOUBLED SIT SLING SEAT

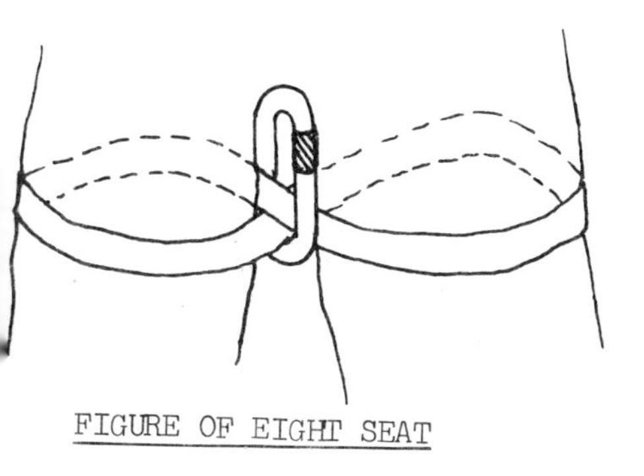

FIGURE OF EIGHT SEAT

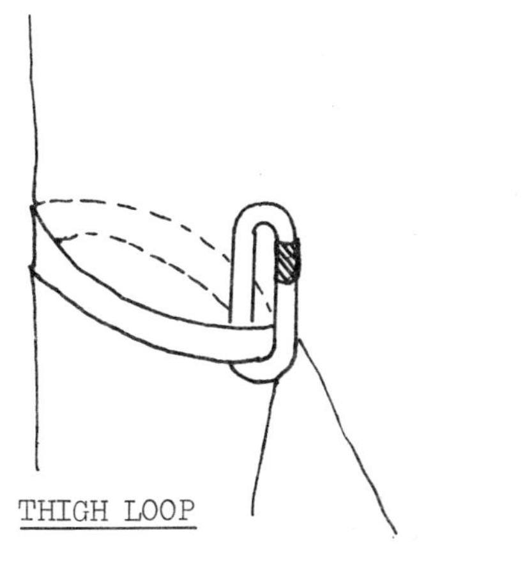

THIGH LOOP

Chest Harnesses

Parisian Baudrier

This harness may be made from a normal eight foot sling passed through one arm and taken round the back and under the other arm. The sling is tied off in the front with a sheet bend thus locking all the parts of the harness.

Crossed Sling Baudrier

This requires a shorter sling and is made by looping the sling over the head and under the arm then twisting a second loop back over the head and under the other arm. It is not as effective as the Parisian Baudrier because it tends to ride up in the front when under load.

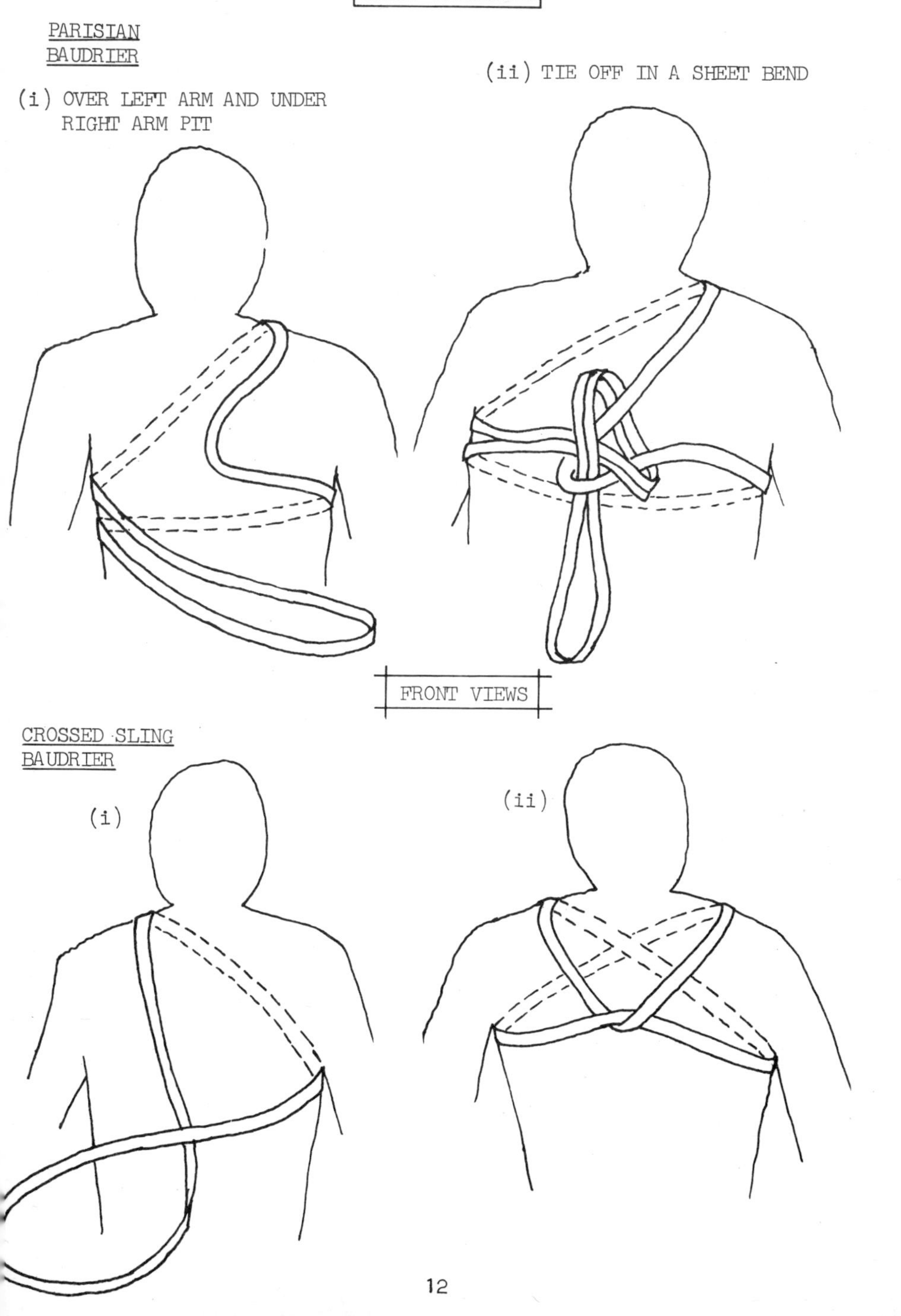
CHEST HARNESSES
PARISIAN
BAUDRIER
(i) OVER LEFT ARM AND UNDER
RIGHT ARM PIT
(ii) TIE OFF IN A SHEET BEND
FRONT VIEWS
CROSSED SLING
BAUDRIER
(i)
(ii)

Full Harnesses

It is possible to construct a full harness using a combination of sit sling and chest harness. The Parisian Baudrier combined with the Dulfer seat makes a comfortable full harness. The Baudrier is tied with an extra long sling giving a long end loop which is clipped into the Dulfer seat, tensioned and tied off in an overhand knot at the suspension point. An adjustable harness can be made by attaching the rope directly to the dulfer seat and fastening the chest harness to the rope with a prusik sling. (Fig. page 15). The prusik sling is tied to the chest harness loop with a sheet bend and is short enough to be easily reached by the climber. The prusik can be slid up and down the rope, thus adjusting the angle of the climber to the lower rope. This is the normal barrow boy rig in a stretcher lower.

Many other combinations are possible using different sit slings, knots, and chest harnesses. It is important to lock off the suspension point of the harness where it is attached to the rope to prevent movement.

IMPROVISED SEAT AND CHEST HARNESS USING TAPE SLINGS

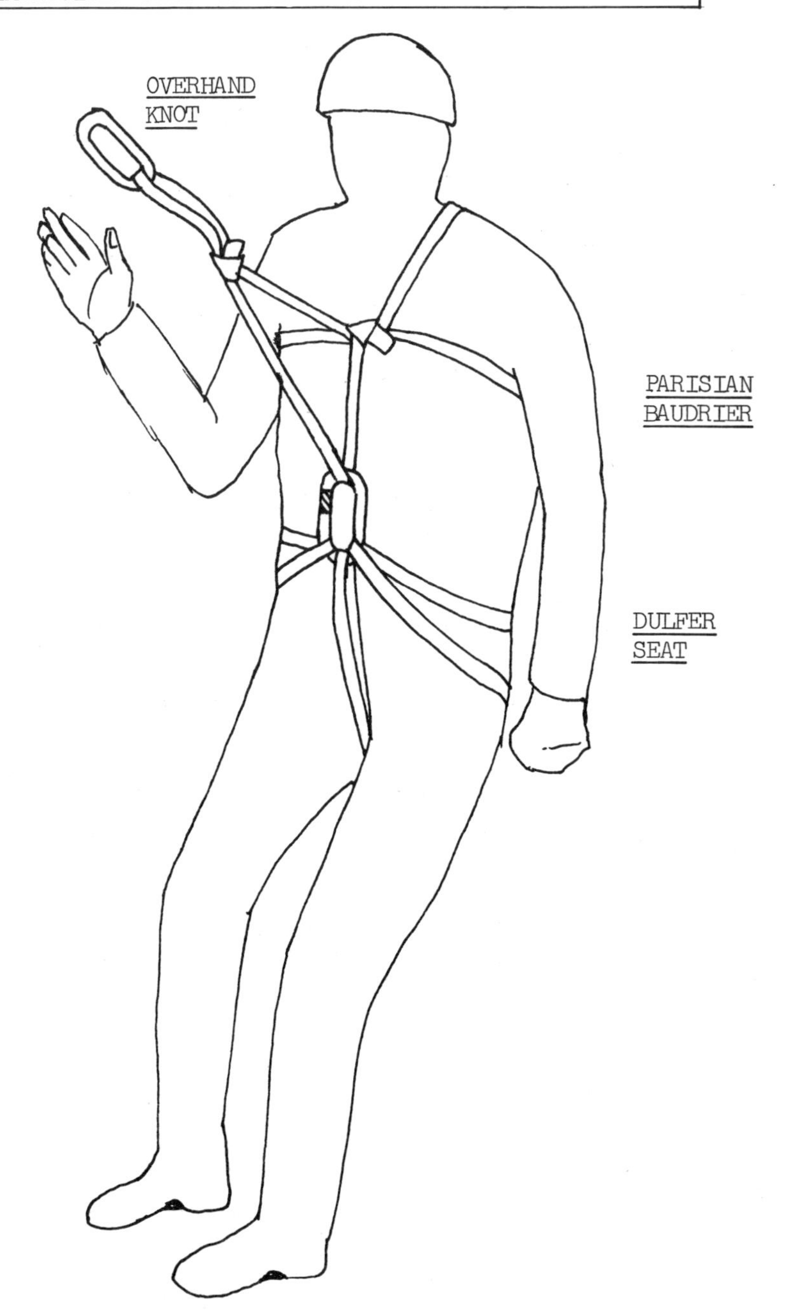

AN ADJUSTABLE SEAT AND CHEST HARNESS USING TAPE SLINGS AND A PRUSIK

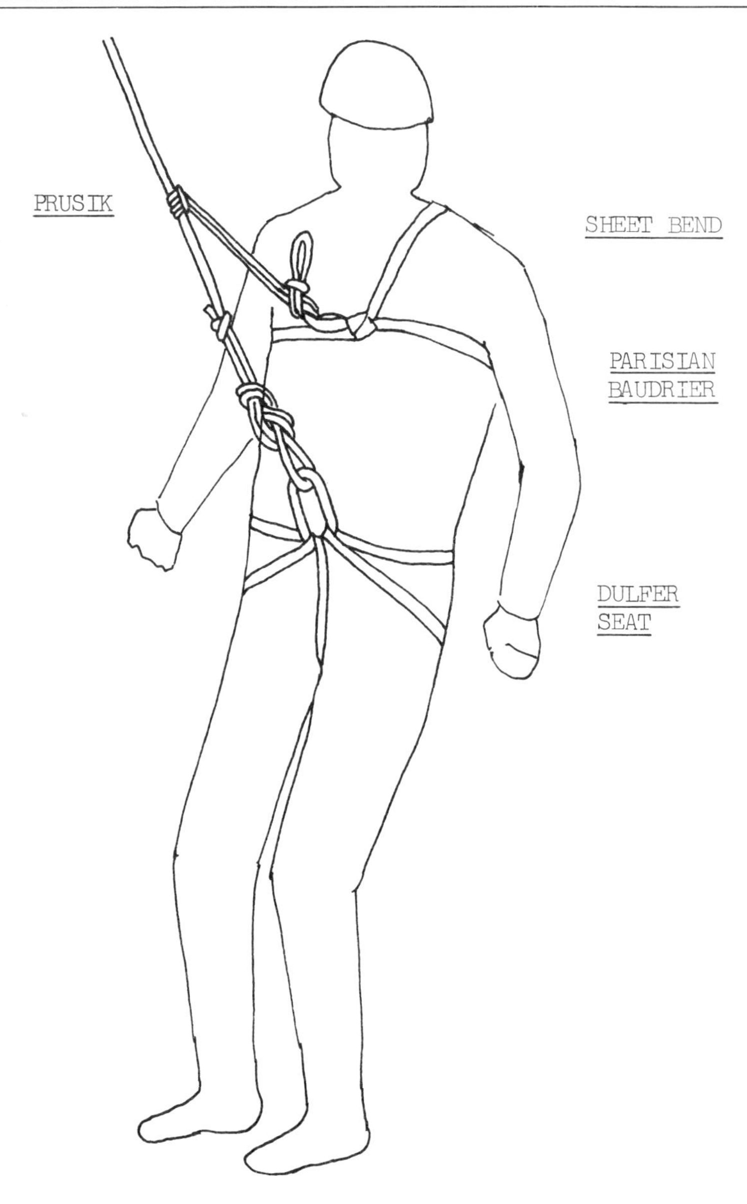

Improvised Tragsitz Using a Climbing Rope Only (Figs. p 17 & 18)

It is possible to construct a tragsitz using only a climbing rope. First take a coil of rope and pay off three coils one side and four coils the other side. Next divide the remaining rope coils evenly into two and split the rope, tying the centre of the split rope coils with line. Take the one end of the three coils and tie a clove hitch on the bottom of one of the rope coils, take the rope across and tie off on the bottom of the other rope coil in the same way, forming a loop. Next take the other end of four coils and tie a clove hitch at the top of the rope coil. Take the rope across in a long loop to the other rope coil and tie off in the same way. Now take the rope back in a short loop to the first coil and fasten in a clove hitch. Take the two long loops, one from the top and one from the bottom, and tie a figure of eight at the end of each. Place casualty in split ropes on carry man's back. The carry man sits astride the bottom ropes and the casualty is held by the top ropes. The short loop is passed under the casualty's arms and across his chest or under his arms and over his head.

IMPROVISED TRAGSITZ USING A CLIMBING ROPE

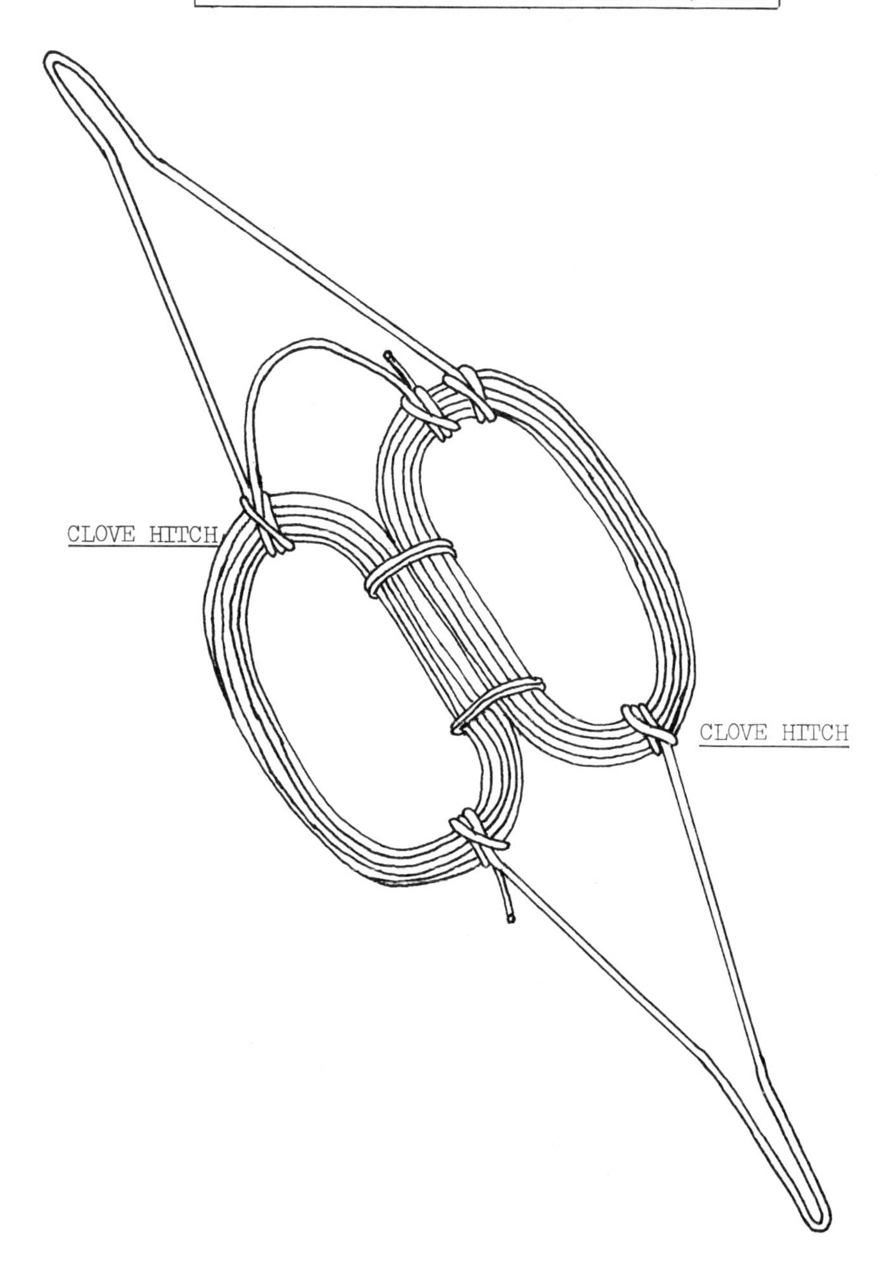

IMPROVISED TRAGSITZ USING A CLIMBING ROPE

Tragsitz

The improvised tragsitz is a method of carrying an injured climber off the cliff on the back of the rescuer. There are many different methods and one is shown here as an example. First rig both casualty and carry man in full harnesses of dulfer seats and parisian baudriers. Attach the carry man to a prusik sling fastened a few feet up the rope. The casualty is carried in a split rope carry tied at the front of the carry man with a piece of line. The prusik sling is adjusted so that the weight of the casualty is taken on the load rope and the carry man provides the legs to keep him away from the rock face. A prusik loop can be attached to the rope for the carry man to hold onto for extra support.

Unless there is a high belay the start of the tragsitz lower exerts considerable strain on the carry man until all the forces are resolved. Once over the edge the carry is comparatively easy if the tragsitz has been correctly adjusted before starting.

IMPROVISED TRAGSITZ LOWER

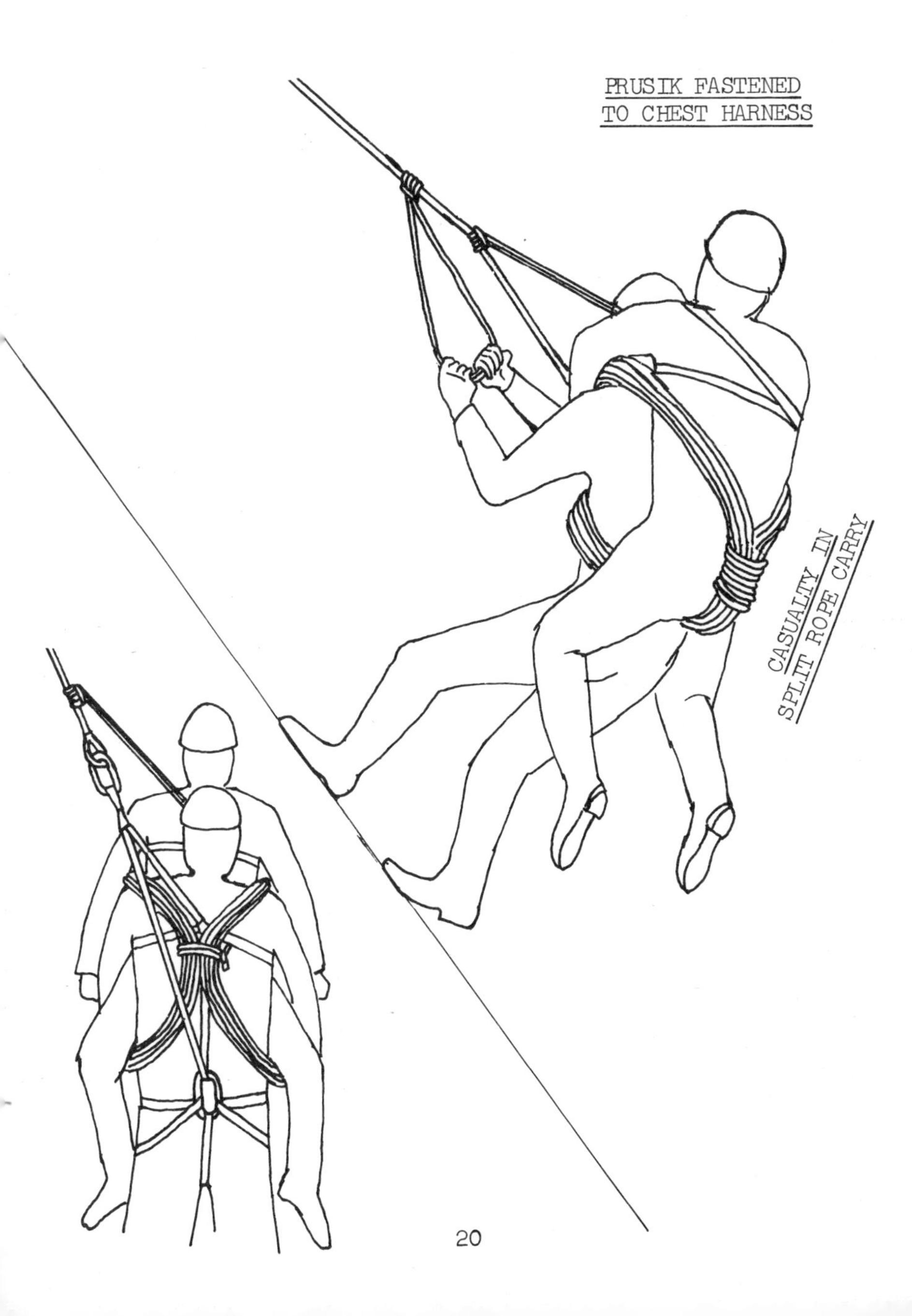

CHAPTER II.

PRUSIK KNOTS AND DEVICES

CHAPTER II.

PRUSIK KNOTS AND DEVICES

Over the last few years there has been an increase in the number of different types of knots and mechanical devices which have tended to replace the conventional sliding friction knot, the prusik. It would be valuable to the climber if an assessment of the existing situation was attempted. At the moment there are at least seven sliding friction knots: the prusik, the karabiner prusik, the Bachmann knot, the Klemheist tied off with the sheet bend (a variation credited J. Zwangwill), the Klemheist knot with karabiner, the Kreuzklem and the Penberthy knot. In addition there are four mechanical devices: Jumars, Heibler, Clog ascenders and Dyna climbs.

All the sliding friction knots follow the same principle - the winding of thinner rope round the main climbing rope to provide friction under load - this is then tied off in various ways. They have varying advantages and disadvantages and the choice of knot can depend upon these as well as the type of task in hand.

The Prusik

The prusik knot is tied with No.1 or No.2 nylon on a No.3 or No.4 rope. The sling is simply wound around the rope and threaded through itself twice, taking care that the second winding is within the first. The knot should be kept symmetrical and there should be no overlapping of the windings otherwise it could slip under the load. Although an effective knot it jams, especially when wet, or subjected to a shock load, or a heavy load and it is difficult to loosen, especially when the operator is under stress or very cold. When No.1 nylon is used it tends to cut into the user and is more susceptible to jamming. Under a shock load a prusik knot tied in No.1 nylon abrades and fuses, and if it is of laid construction, kinks up, knotting the strands. Such a situation developed when a climber abseiling with a prusik loop attached to the rope as a safeguard, lost control and descended rapidly: he was saved, but only just, by his prusik. A number two prusik is much stronger and safer and is less liable to act in this way. The great advantage of the prusik knot is that it is simple to tie and can be attached with one hand. This requires practice. the easiest way is to roll the knot fastening the prusik sling around the main rope twice and pull it through itself. This may be useful when hanging free on the rope after a fall or tying off the load rope when someone has fallen off.

Prusik with Karabiner

The prusik knot may be tied around a karabiner which provides a handhold facilitating the moving of the knot and making it less susceptible to jamming.

The Klemheist Knot

The sling is wound around the main rope in a spiral and then threaded through itself - the amount of friction can be controlled by increasing or decreasing the number of turns. This knot may be improved by tying off with sheet bend, a development originated by John Zwangwill. Although requiring time and two hands to tie this improved version it is very successful and less liable to jam and easier to loosen than the prusik.

SLIDING FRICTION KNOTS

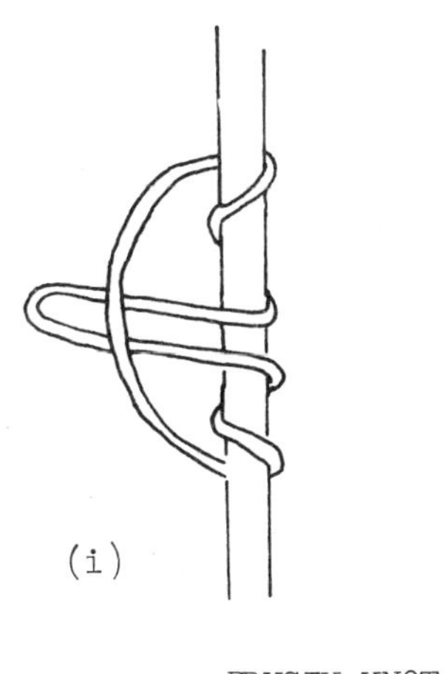

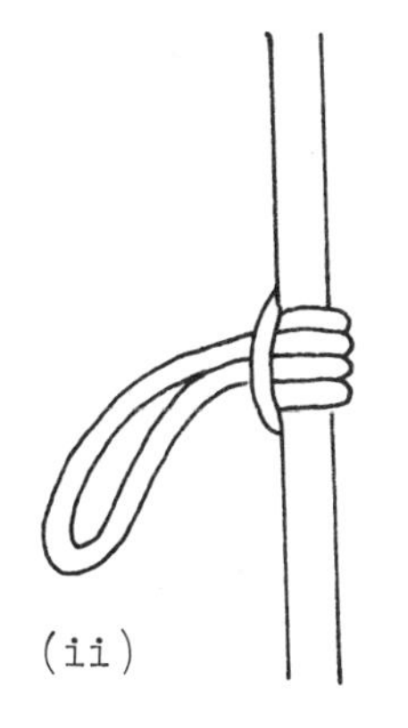

PRUSIK KNOT

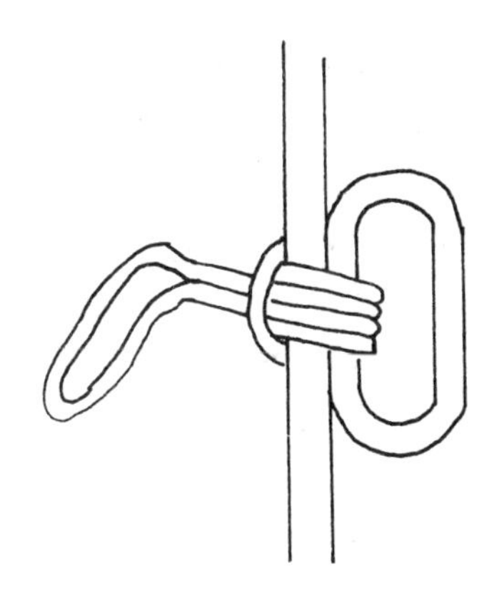

PRUSIK KNOT TIED WITH A KARABINER

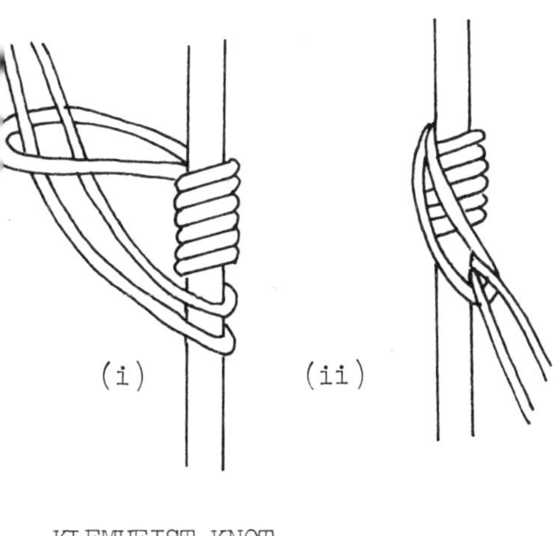

KLEMHEIST KNOT

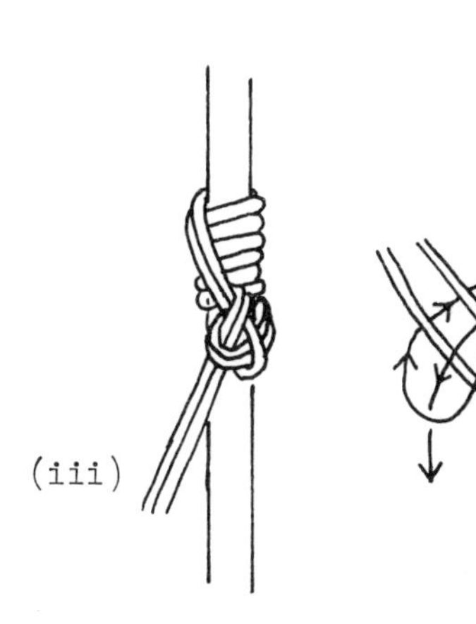

KLENHEIST KNOT TIED OFF WITH A SHEET BEND

Bachmann

In this knot the sling is clipped into a karabiner and wound round the main rope and the back bar of the karabiner in a descending spiral. The friction can be controlled by the number of turns. This is a superior knot to the prusik as it works better on wet and icy ropes, although it has to be tied using two hands. This knot is especially useful in pulley systems used for hoisting casualties.

The Klemheist Knot with Karabiner

This is simply the knot tied around the main rope and the karabiner. It is very effective and easier to release as the karabiner provides a secure handhold.

The Kreuzklem

This is tied in the reversed direction to the Klemheist - the sling is wound around and up the main rope once and threaded back through itself. This is a simple and effective knot which is easily loosened by pushing the end of the looped sling with th thumb.

The Penberthy Knot

The Penberthy knot is tied with a length of rope wound in a spiral around the climbing rope and tied with a bowline which is adjusted so as to tighten the spiral turns of the rope. The two ends of the sling are then joined in the conventional way, i.e., fisherman's or double fishermans. This is a very effectiv knot which does not jam, but does take time to tie. A quick improvised method of tying; a type of Penberthy knot is to weight a sling with a karabiner and spin this around the rope and threac the sling through the karabiner.

SLIDING FRICTION KNOTS

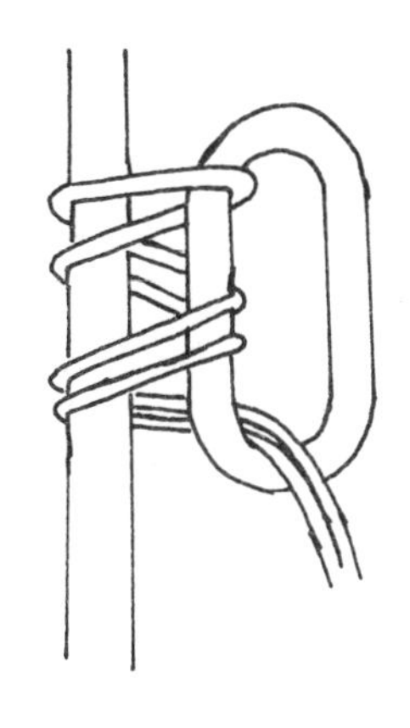

BACHMANN KNOT

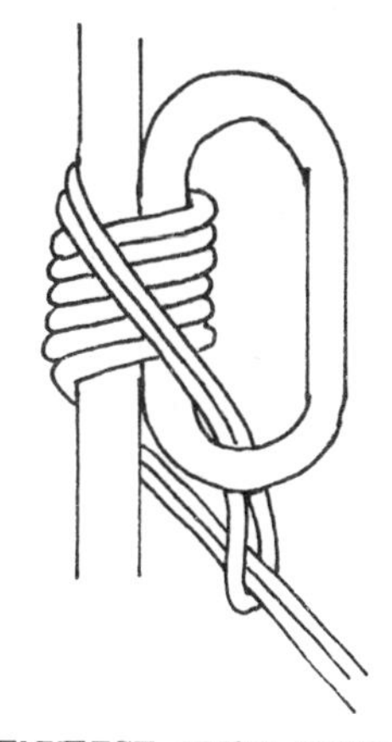

KLEMHEIST KNOT TIED WITH A KARABINER

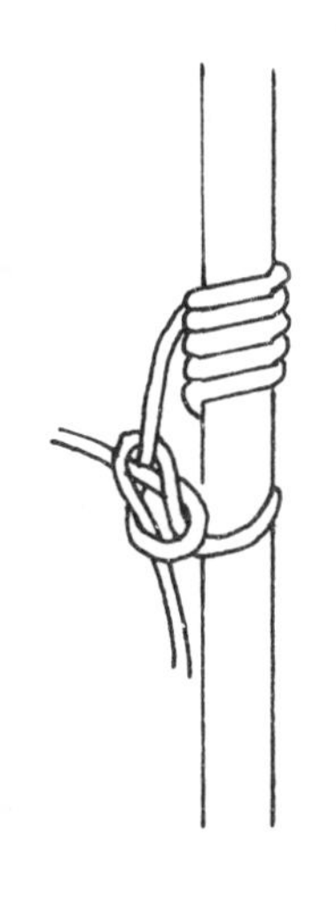

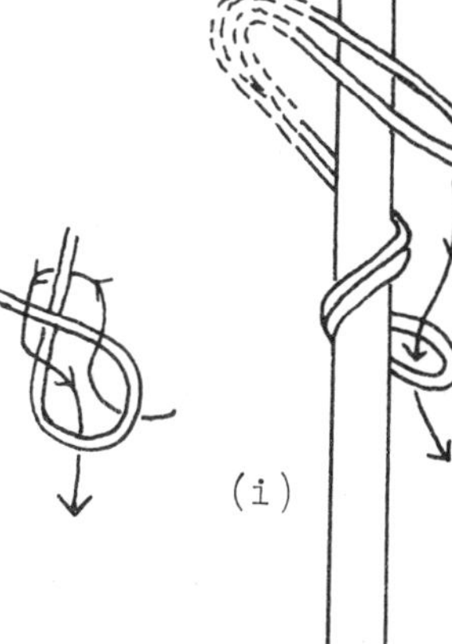

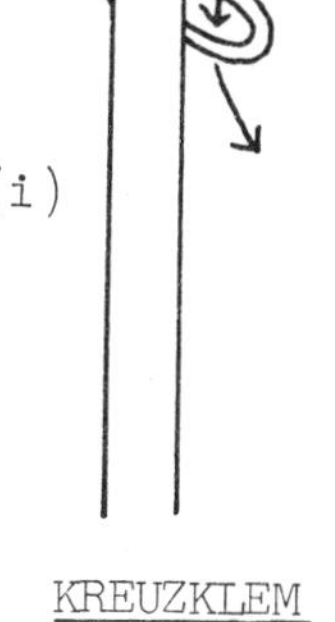

ENBERTHY KNOT TIED WITH A LENGTH F ROPE WHICH IS THEN JOINED

KREUZKLEM

Mechanical Devices

In general mechanical prusiking devices or clamps are superior in use to improvised knots and karabiner combinations. However, they do have disadvantages which are worthy of consideration:
(i) They are expensive; it is doubtful that such an investment is necessary unless you contemplate doing a great deal of prusiking.
(ii) Unlike the prusik knots they cannot be used on a doubled rope e.g., for safeguarding a person abseiling.
(iii) They are extra items of equipment to carry and have one use as opposed to slings and karabiners which are multi-purpose.
(iv) As mechanical devices they may break or malfunction due to fatigue or wear.

Apart from these general considerations the different clamps have specific advantages and disadvantages which are inherent in their design. They all have one thing in common; they must be operated correctly to obtain the maximum advantage.

Jumar Clamps

Although the most expensive and the largest of the prusikers, the Jumar clamps are the most effective. They consist of a rectangular metal handle with a semi-circular sleeve through which the rope runs. The rope is kept in place by a spring loaded clamp with small teeth which bite into the rope. When a load is placed on the Jumar the clamp is forced up and into the rope in the sleeve. A spring loaded safety trigger acting upwards prevents the clamp from opening too far when being moved. The Jumar is easily operated with one hand - to place it onto the rope depress the safety trigger with the middle finger and the spring loaded clamp with the thumb and clip onto the rope. Sometimes the Jumar may appear to jam on descent and the spring clamp cannot be depressed; in this instance the prusiker must be moved up a little

JUMAR CLAMPS

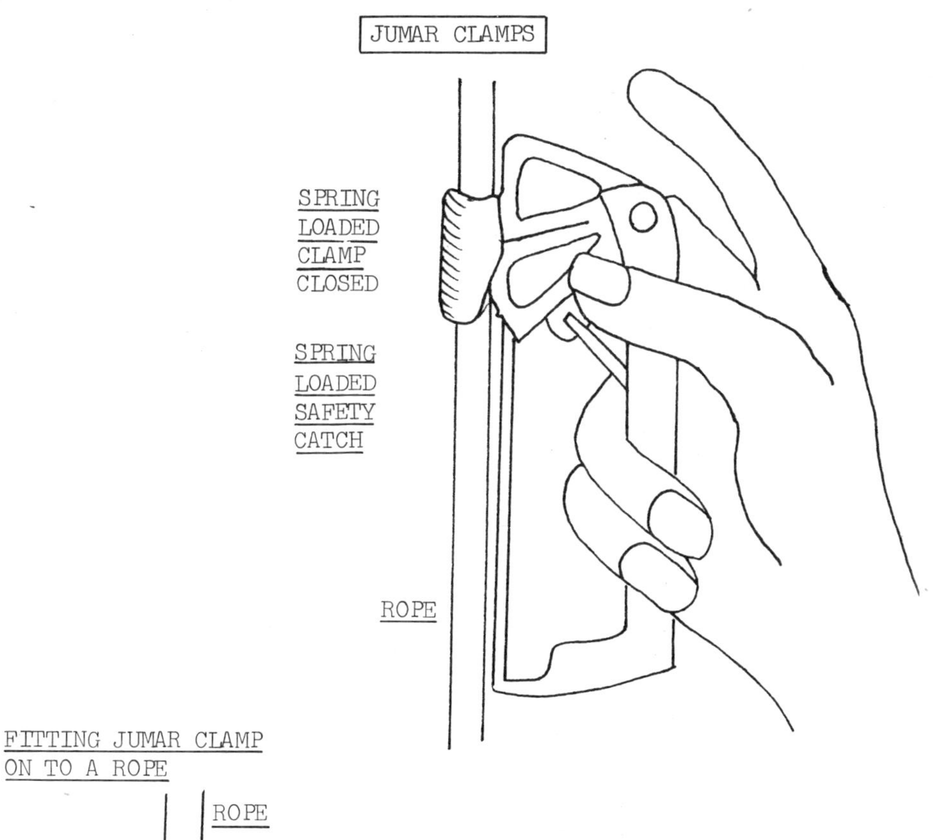

FITTING JUMAR CLAMP
ON TO A ROPE

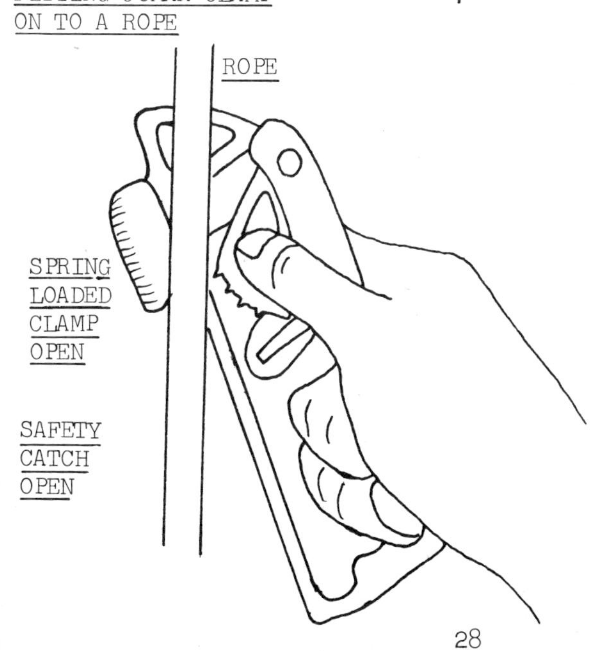

to release the spring clamp. When moving the jumars avoid an overlap as they may jam as one is forced at an angle to the rope. Under cold icy conditions the teeth of the spring clamp may be filled in with ice and may slip on an icy rope. In this situation the teeth must be cleared out with a sharp instrument.

Heibler Clamps

The Heibler clamp consists of a U shaped sleeve with one arm of the U extended as a bar on its upper side and the other arm serving as a base for a spring loaded lever. When weight is applied to the end of the lever it pivots up, locking the rope in the sleeve and tilts the clamp, causing the rope to bend. When not under load the lever is kept in position by a spring. They can be attached and removed from the climbing rope with one hand and are simple to operate.

Although effective as prusikers the Heibler clamps have a tendency to slip off the rope if subject to any lateral forces or twisting. The diagram illustrates how easily the rope can come out from the bottom of the clamp. When using the clamp always keep the thumb around the clamp until it is under tension. The later models have been fitted with a safety clip which when in position prevents the squeezing of the lever too far forward to allow the rope to slip out. Even with this modification,however, care should always be exercised when using Heiblers.

ATTACHMENT OF THE HIEBLER PRUSIKER TO THE CLIMBING ROPE

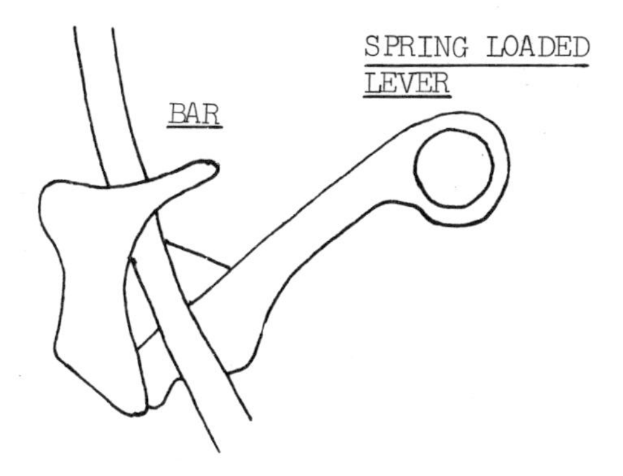

INSERT THE ROPE INTO
THE TOP OF THE CLAMP
BEHIND THE BAR

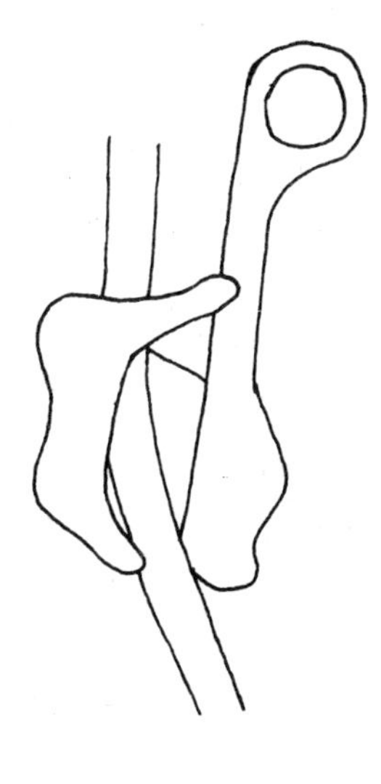

SQUEEZE THE LEVER
UP AGAINST THE
SPRING AND SLOT
THE ROPE INTO THE
BOTTOM OF CLAMP

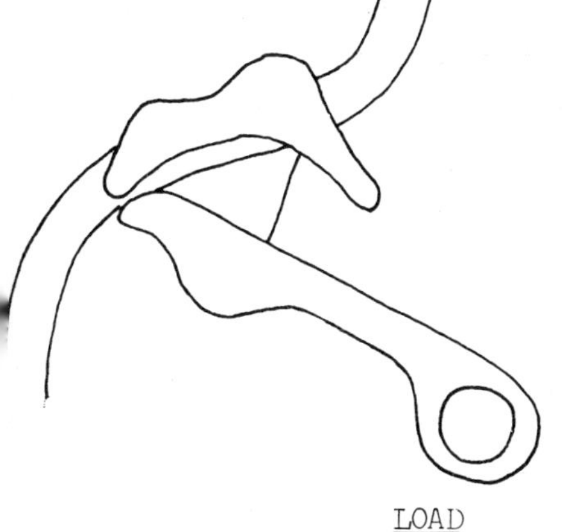

CLAMP IN THE LOCKING
POSITION UNDER LOAD

Clog Ascender

The clog ascender consists of an alloy base plate, triangular in shape, with the apex bent over in a U, from which is pivoted a spring loaded lever. The base of the triangular plate is curved over into a U sleeve to accommodate the rope which is held in place by the lever. The front of the lever is serrated to grip the rope more effectively. Below the pivot of the lever there is a hole large enough for a karabiner. When the karabiner is clipped in, it prevents the lever from opening and thereby acts as a safety catch. It is, therefore, impossible to remove or to replace the ascender on the rope when the karabiner is in place. In certain situations this could prove awkward. The clog functions effectively although under certain conditions it has slight tendency to slip, especially when the load is not acting vertically downwards on the clamp. On the later models this defect has been remedied.

The Dyna Climb

This is a smaller version of the Clog and is convenient and easily carried in a pocket for an emergency. It does however have the same characteristics, including the tendency to slip.

OPERATION OF THE HIEBLER PRUSIKER

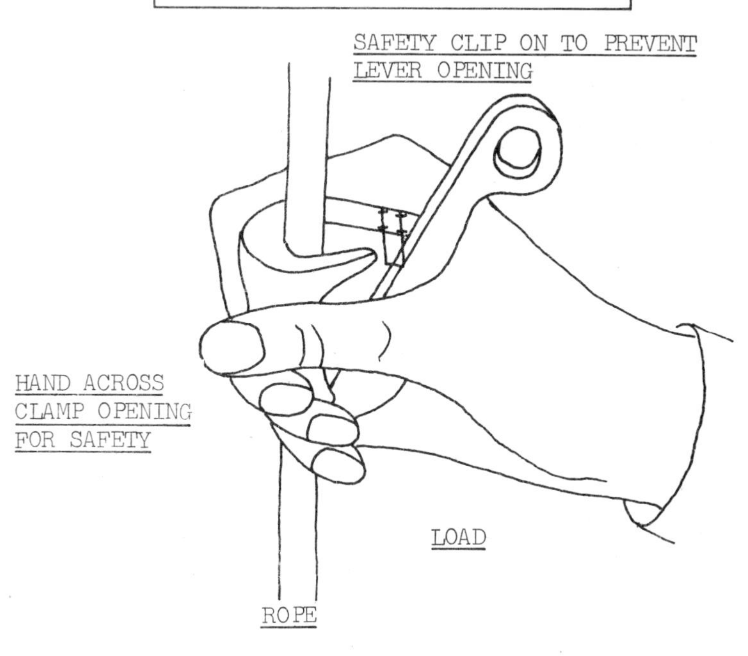

OPERATION OF THE DYNACLIMB

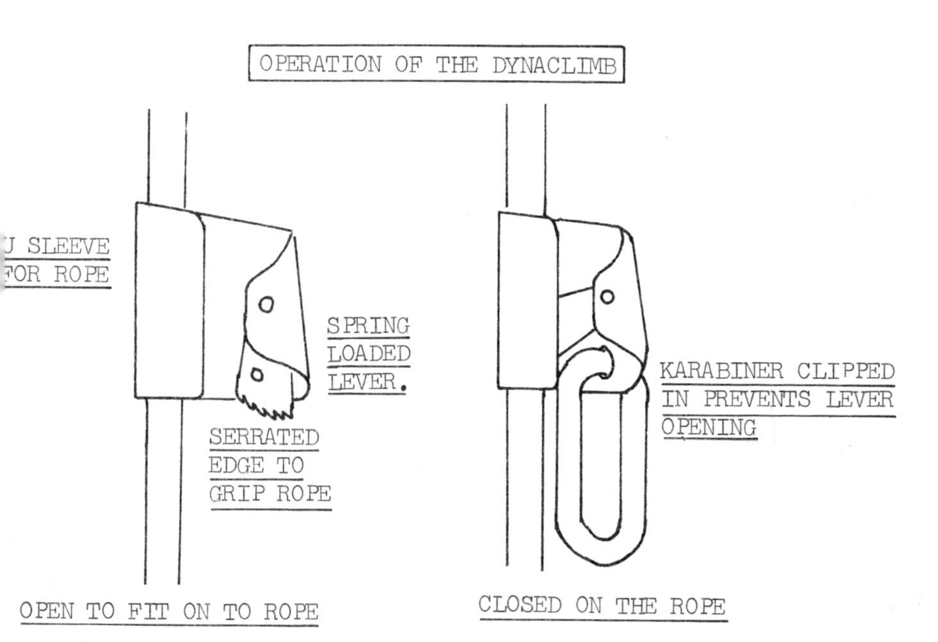

CHAPTER III

H O I S T I N G

CHAPTER III

HOISTING

There is little doubt that of all the self rescue techniques hoisting is the most difficult and the most strenuous. It should, therefore, whenever possible, be avoided and some other technique employed e.g. lowering to the bottom or traversing off. The degree of difficulty experienced depends upon the number of people available and the ability of the casualty to assist himself. The situations may be classified as follows:

(a) Self-Hoisting - using prusik slings or ascenders a person can climb up a rope. There is a wide range of different methods operating on the same principles.

(b) Assisted Hoisting - where assistance is given from above as in the two in one karabiner pulley hoist or the stirrup hoist.

(c) Unassisted Hoist - where all the work is done at the top by the rescuers. This is naturally the most strenuous of the hoists. The Yosemite Lift and the two in one Bachmann hoist are examples of the unassisted hoist.

(a) Self-Hoist

Methods of easing the strain on the waistline when hanging free.

The first essential if one is not wearing some kind of seat or harness is to take weight of the waistline off the chest. This may be accomplished in a variety of ways:

(i) Clip a sling, which is slightly shorter than the waist to foot distance, into the waistline karabiner and stand on it. This immediately takes some of the weight off the waist. The length of the sling is critical and should be determined by practice in a safe situation. In an emergency, a long sling can be shortened by knotting, or several short slings can be joined together.

(ii) Tie on to the rope four feet or more from the end and tie a foot loop into the free end of the rope. This can be tucked away until it is required.

METHODS OF EASING THE STRAIN ON THE WAIST WHEN HANGING FREE

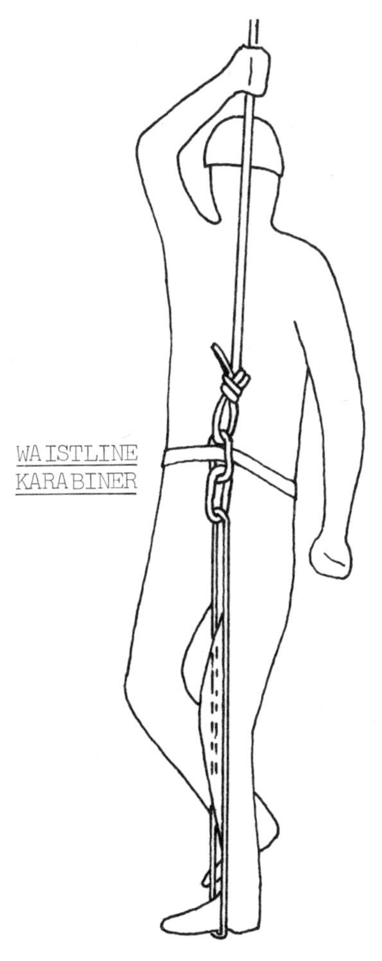

(i) USING A SLING AND KRAB CLIPPED INTO THE WAISTLINE KARABINER

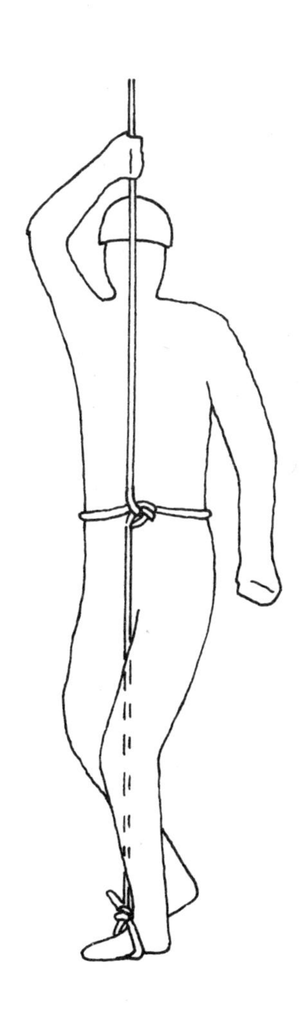

(ii) TYING ON, LEAVING ENOUGH ROPE SPARE FOR A FOOT LOO

(iii) Fasten a prusik sling to the rope, whenever, you think you are in a situation that merits this precaution. The sling is passed through the waistline and tucked away in a pocket. This is the conventional method and when crossing crevassed areas the climber generally attaches two or three prusiks to his climbing rope. Once he has taken the weight off his waist he is in a position to ascend the rope using his prusik slings.

(iv) An ingenious method of making a quick improvised seat has been developed by Australian rock climbers and is known as the "Baboon Hang". The climber turns upside down to take the weight off the chest and holds this position by trapping a leg behind the climbing rope. A short sling is put over both legs and pulled up to the buttocks. The length of this sling is important and it should be worked out before hand, although an adjustable sling could be used e.g. tied with a sheet bend. A long sling could be knotted to the required length by tying an overhand. The climber then sits upright by pulling up on the rope; he is now in a ready made seat with a leg loop held either side of the climbing rope.

Once the initial strain is taken off the waist by one of the methods outlined above the climber can prepare his method of ascending the rope in relative comfort.

METHODS OF EASING THE STRAIN ON THE WAISTLINE WHEN HANGING FREE

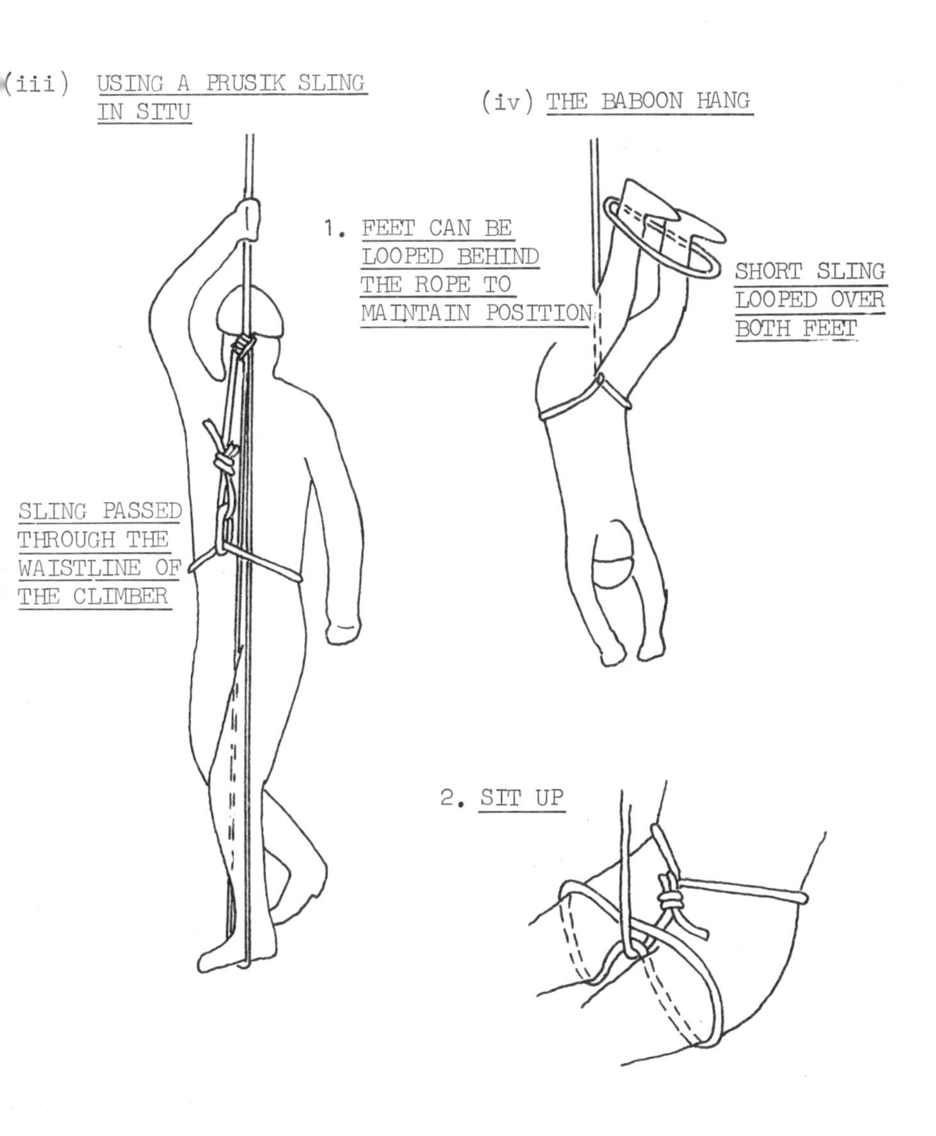

Prusiking with two slings

It is possible to prusik with two long slings passed through the waist line or, better still, a chest harness which is attached to the feet with a larks foot. The climber is held upright and into the rope by either loop when it is held under tension. The climber transfers his weight alternately from one to the other moving up the unloaded sling each time and then stepping up. If the prusik loops are attached to the climbing rope below the level of the chest the chest harness can be clipped to the prusiking rope with a karabiner keeping the climber close to the rope which is always under tension.

Another method, which is probably more comfortable, is to prusik with a sit sling and foot loop. The sit sling is attached to a short prusik and the foot loop is long if it is fastened to the rope above the sit sling prusik Fig (ii) and short if it is fastened below Fig (i). The climber sits, unweights the foot loop and moves it up the rope; he then steps up unweights the sit sling prusik which is moved up the rope to a higher position. This method has the advantage of leaving the climber in a comparatively comfortable resting position in a sit sling with a free leg to push off against the cliff face.

TWO METHODS OF PRUSIKING WITH SIT SLING AND FOOT LOOP

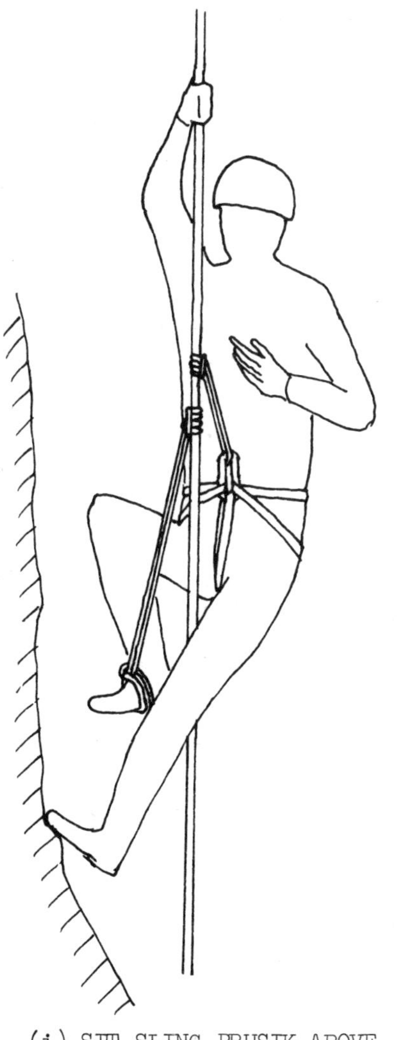

(i) SIT SLING PRUSIK ABOVE SHORT FOOT LOOP PRUSIK

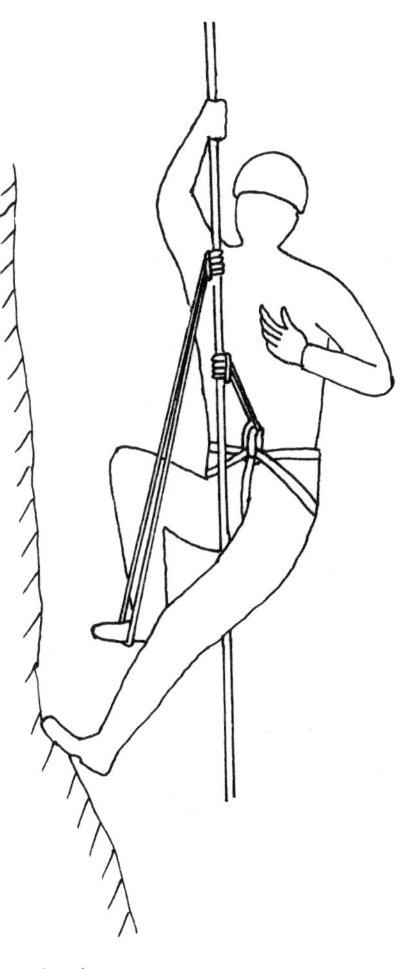

(ii) SIT SLING PRUSIK BELOW LONG FOOT LOOP PRUSIK

The disadvantage of the sit sling method is the tendency to turn upside down as the centre of gravity is above the attachment point. This is especially noticeable on a free prusik where there is no cliff face to prop the leg; or where a load may be carried on the back. The load could be carried slung on a rope from the waist below the centre of gravity, thus increasing stability. A combined chest harness/sit sling could be used thus raising the attachment point above the centre of gravity. This is possibly the most comfortable method of prusiking. Additional security may be provided by securing a short sling from the foot loop prusik to the chest harness, thus safeguarding the climber in the event of failure of his chest prusik. This is particularly advisable when using mechanical prusikers. A further precaution when using mechanical prusikers is to fasten a safety prusik loop above the ascender and attach it to the chest.

There are other combinations and methods of prusiking with which the climber can experiment, adapting the most satisfactory method for his own use.

Prusiking with three slings

The classic method of climbing a rope is to utilise three prusik loops, one for each foot and one for the chest. The foot loops may be tied off with a larks foot to prevent them falling off the feet when not under tension. The chest loops may be clipped into the waistline karabiner which is moved to the back for this purpose, or it may be tied off at the chest in an overhand knot for additional security. The climber moves one prusik loop at a time and should develop a rhythm especially with the chest prusik of moving up and pushing the prusik up at the same time. Always ensure the load is released before attempting to move the prusik loop up. The length of the prusik loops is important. The chest loop should be shorter than the foot loop. Since individuals vary in size and proportion it would be adviseable to experiment in a controlled situation to discover the optimum length of slings. Slings tied with the sheet bend can easily be adjusted in length or they may be shortened by tying overhand or figure of eight knots. Short slings may be lengthened by looping two or three together. The facility for making do with the equipment available is really the crux of improvisation in rescue.

SELF HOIST WITH THREE PRUSIK LOOPS

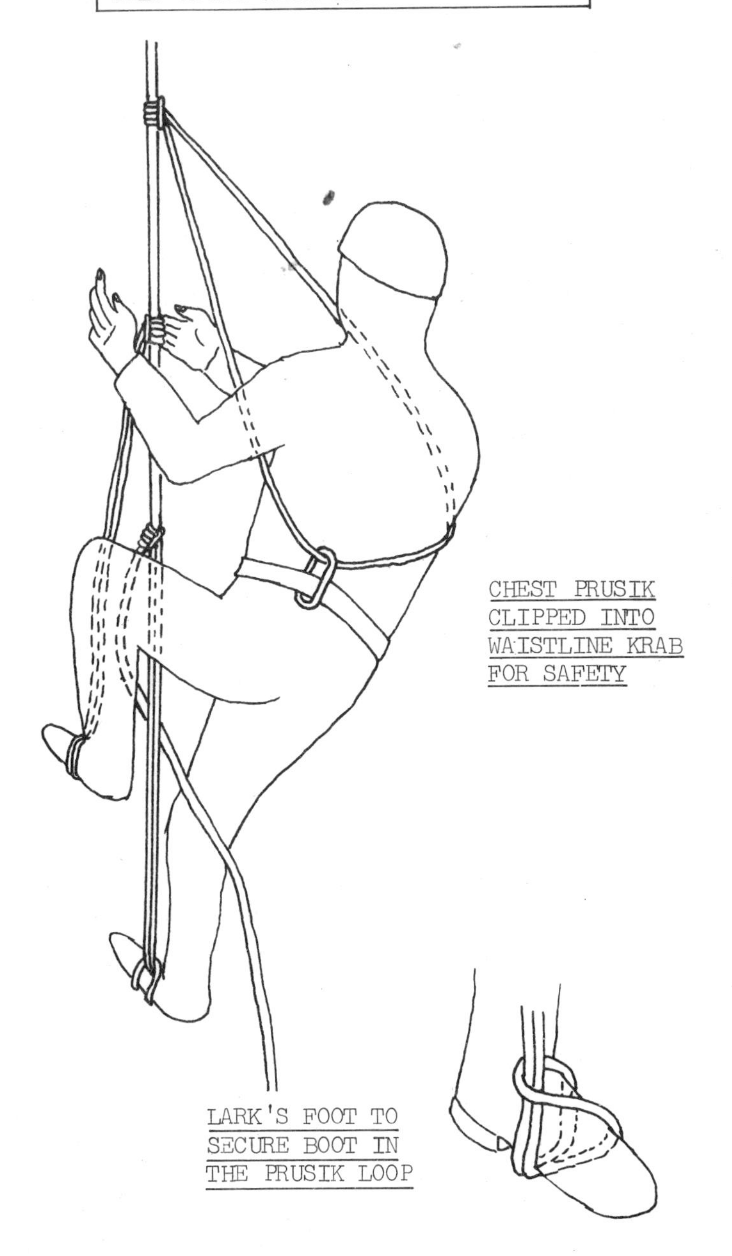

(b) Assisted Hoists

In certain situations it is possible for the people above to give assistance to the person below.

(i) Straight Hoist

On some occasions over a short distance it is possible to pull a person up using a locking prusik and a shoulder belay. A prusik is attached to the climbing rope just below the belayer's waist and the shoulder belay position is adopted with the load rope under the arm and over the opposite shoulder. To lift, bend the knees take in the rope tight and straighten the legs using the powerful leg muscles to lift the casualty. As the rope is hoisted slide the prusik forward to take the load and repeat. This is a strenuous method and can only be used with strong hoisters and light casualties and where the casualty can assist by using holds on the rock face.

(ii) Assisted Stirrup Hoist

In this method two ropes with sliding foot loops are dropped to the casualty who passes them through his chest harness and around the inside of his thighs to fasten them to the feet. Both ropes are passed through prusik knots at the top. The casualty alternately shifts his weight from one foot to the other thus unloading a rope which can be pulled up through the prusik the distance of a high step. On stepping up the other rope is unloaded and the

(ii) ASSISTED STIRRUP HOIST

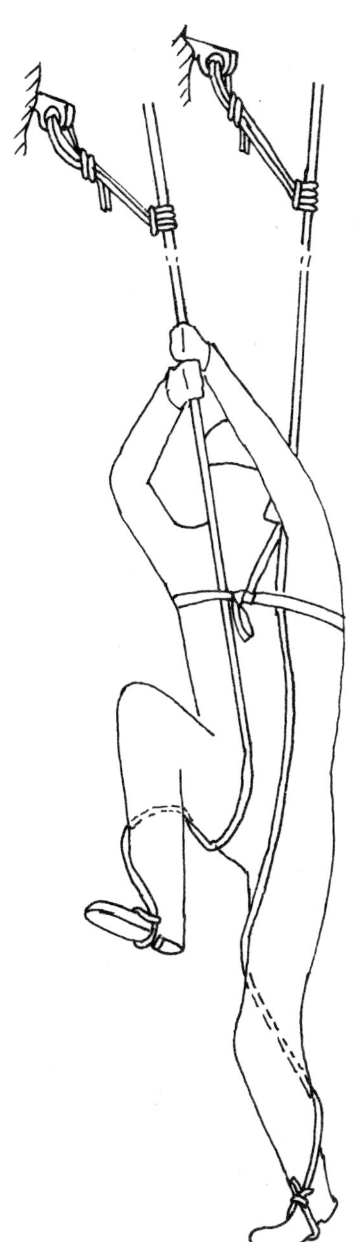

operation repeated. Clear communication between the casualty and hoister is essential for a smooth hoist. A similar operation may be performed with the casualty standing in a prusik loop attached to his climbing rope with a foot loop rope lowered to him. In a crevasse rescue situation the second foot loop rope could be the other end of his climbing rope. If the casualty had an injured ankle but was otherwise alright a method using a sit-sling and foot loop could be employed with the casualty using his good leg to step up and the sit-sling as a resting stage.

(iii) Two in One Karabiner Hoist with Casualty Assisting

This method of hoisting is quite simple and requires little extra equipment. The top man of a pair of roped climbers clips the climbing rope through an anchored karabiner and drops a loop of the rope with a sit-sling and karabiner attached to the lower man. The lower man puts on the sit-sling and clips the karabiner through the loop of rope which now forms an "S" from himself, up to the anchored krab pulley, down to his sit-sling and finally up to the top man. This end of the rope may be locked off on a prusik fastened to a piton. The top man hoists using a shoulder belay, straight back and bent legs pushing the prusik forward as he lifts to lock off the rope. The lower man can pull on the rope running down to his sit-sling karabiner to assist the hoist. It is possible, however, for the top man to hoist without using assistance from the lower man apart from walking up the face.

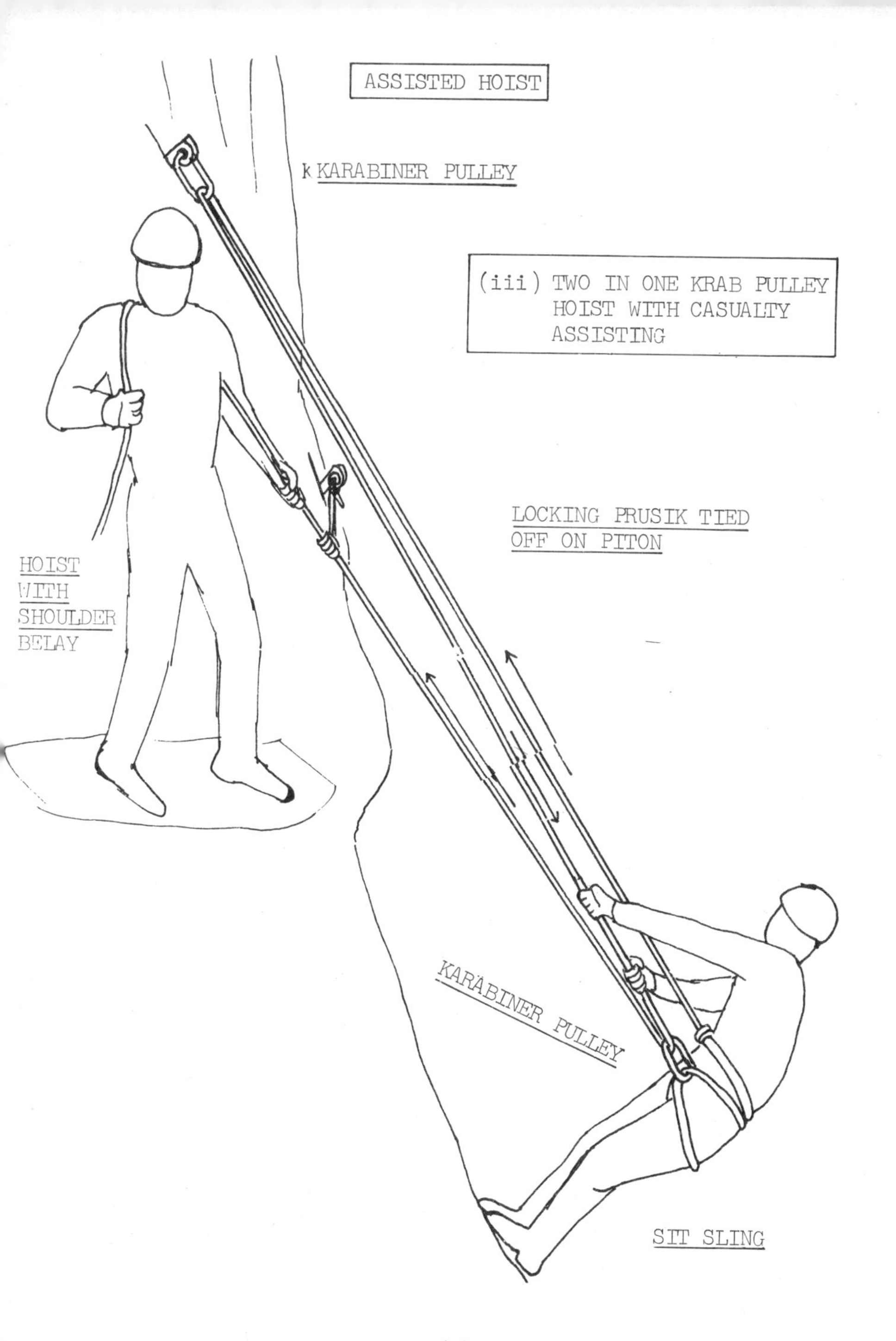
ASSISTED HOIST
KARABINER PULLEY
(iii) TWO IN ONE KRAB PULLEY HOIST WITH CASUALTY ASSISTING
LOCKING PRUSIK TIED OFF ON PITON
HOIST WITH SHOULDER BELAY
KARÄBINER PULLEY
SIT SLING

(c) Unassisted Hoist

(i) Yosemite Lift

The Yosemite lift is a method where the hoister uses his own body weight to assist in the operation. The rope is passed through an anchored karabiner which acts as a pulley and a locking prusik or inverted ascender, tied off at the top and bottom, is attached to the loaded side. On the other side of the karabiner pulley a prusik foot loop is attached. The load is lifted by pumping with the foot and pulling with the hands. As the foot stirrup is pressed down and the rope lifted the locking prusik is slid forward to hold the load. The foot stirrup can then be loosened off and slid up the rope in preparation for the next hoist. It is important that the foot prusik is pumped in the same line as the load rope to obtain the maximum mechanical advantage.

(i) YOSEMITE LIFT

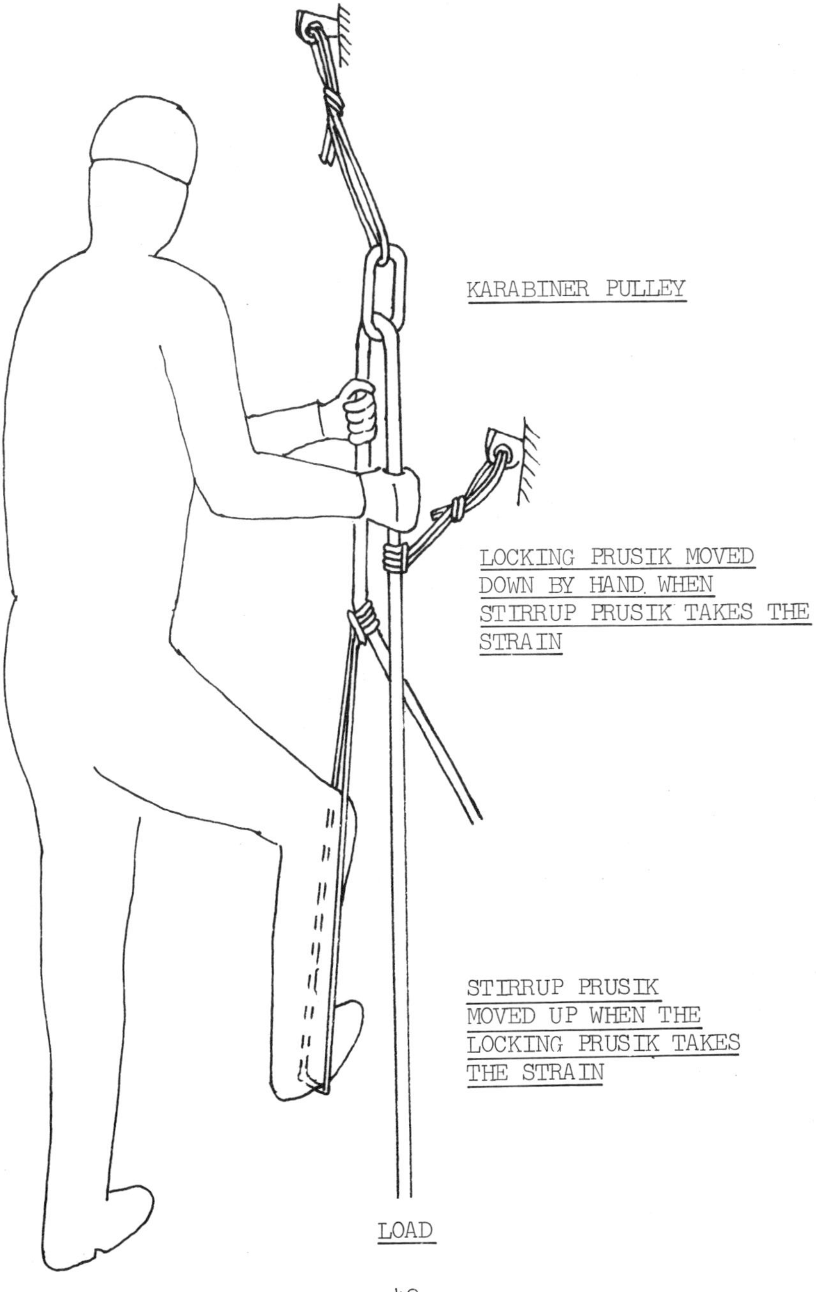

KARABINER PULLEY

LOCKING PRUSIK MOVED DOWN BY HAND WHEN STIRRUP PRUSIK TAKES THE STRAIN

STIRRUP PRUSIK MOVED UP WHEN THE LOCKING PRUSIK TAKES THE STRAIN

LOAD

(ii) Two in One Bachmann Hoist

This method makes use of a one way clutch arrangement using a Bachmann knot. The rope is passed through an anchored karabiner which acts as a pulley, and an inverted Bachmann knot is fastened on the load rope side and tied off to a separate anchor point close by. A short prusik loop is then attached to the load rope and the free rope is clipped to it with a karabiner. When the free rope is pulled the Bachmann is jammed against the top pulley karabiner and the rope runs free pulling the bottom prusik up towards the rope anchor. On releasing the free rope the Bachmann comes under tension and locks off the load rope allowing the prusik knot to be slid forward down the load rope in preparation for another hoist. The Bachmann must be anchored close to the pulley karabiner to avoid excessive play on the transfer of load from the pulley karabiner to the Bachmann. It may help if there are two pulley karabiners together giving a longer circumference; they should if possible be smaller than the karabiner on which the Bachmann knot is tied. The further forward the bottom prusik can be pushed the better, as it gives a longer pull with sustained momentum.

(ii) THE TWO IN ONE BACHMANN HOIST

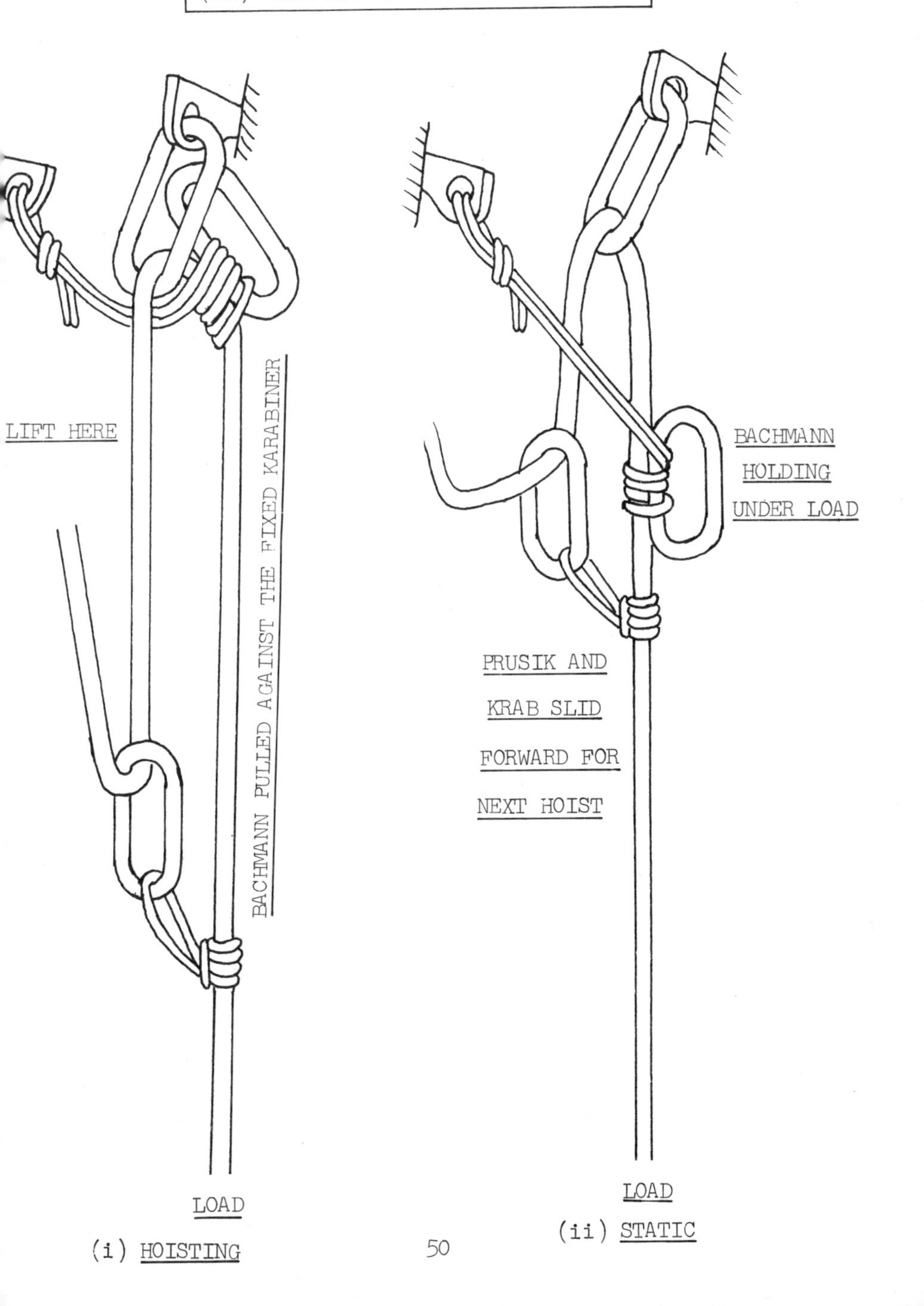

Karabiner Pulley Hoists

There are many combinations of karabiner pulley hoists and one opposite is shown as an example. It is important to remember that after a two in one advantage factor such as increased friction of rope over karabiners and decreased distance hoisted tend to nullify the increased mechanical advantage. The friction of the rope running over the rock face and the position of the available belay points are factors which must be considered when setting up a rescue hoist. The question one must always ask is "what will happen if ....?"

KARABINER PULLEY HOIST

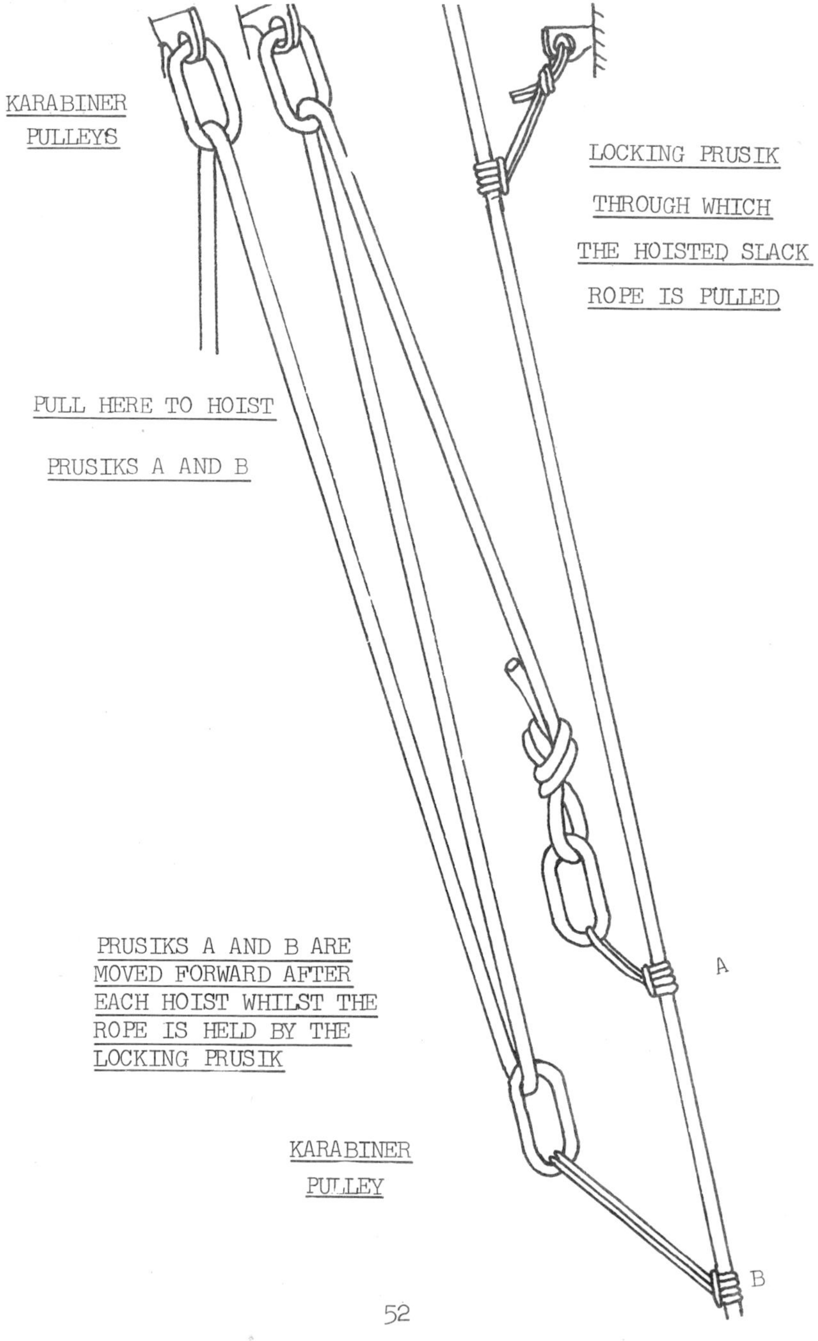

KARABINER PULLEYS

LOCKING PRUSIK THROUGH WHICH THE HOISTED SLACK ROPE IS PULLED

PULL HERE TO HOIST PRUSIKS A AND B

A

PRUSIKS A AND B ARE MOVED FORWARD AFTER EACH HOIST WHILST THE ROPE IS HELD BY THE LOCKING PRUSIK

KARABINER PULLEY

B

Crevasse Rescue

The methods described in this chapter are those often used in crevasse rescue and a few comments should be made concerning the complications arising from this type of rescue.

(i) The rope cuts into the edge of the crevasse which is often overhung.

   (a) Cut away the edge of crevasse if possible.

   (b) Pad the rope with rucksacks or spare ice axe, skis etc. to prevent this.

   (c) Attach another rope to the rescue rope with a karabiner and belay it onto an anchor point on the other side of the crevasse. Tension the rope until it pulls the rescue rope away from the crevasse edge and fasten with a hitch tied on the bight which can be released under load.

   (d) Use etriers clipped together since they do not bite into the crevasse wall as easily. If no etriers are available a rope ladder may be fashioned out of loops.

(ii) The provision of rescue anchor points - see chapter on belays.

When crossing crevassed areas:

   (a) Always move in groups of 3 or more

   (b) Always roped with each member carrying 1/3 of the rope length for rescue purposes.

   (c) Always have 3 prusiks attached to the rope ready for use.

Rescue of an Unconscious Person Hanging Free on a Waistline Attachment

This situation is a serious one as there is little time in which to carry out the rescue before the person dies from the constricting effect of the rope on his chest. The major difficulty is very often in reaching the person to administer assistance. One method would be to attach an inverted jumar or inverted Bachmann knot to the rope and weight it with a rucksack or some pitons. Attach a back rope to the loaded jumar and allow it to slide down the rope to the hanging climber. The jumar holds under load and the climber can be pulled into the side.

It is essential to take the weight of the climber off his waistline and to transfer it to a sit-sling or chest harness. To accomplish this attach a short prusik loop to the rope above the hanging climber and clip a karabiner into this to act as a pulley. Place the unconscious climber in a sit-sling and attach it to a long sling which is passed through the pulley karabiner and attached to an etrier lifting the hanging climber up into the sit-sling and releasing the weight on the waistline. The sit-sling is then clipped to another prusik attached to the load rope. A chest harness may be attached in the same way.

A METHOD OF EASING THE STRAIN ON A PERSON HANGING UNCONSCIOUS FROM A WAIST LINE ATTACHMENT

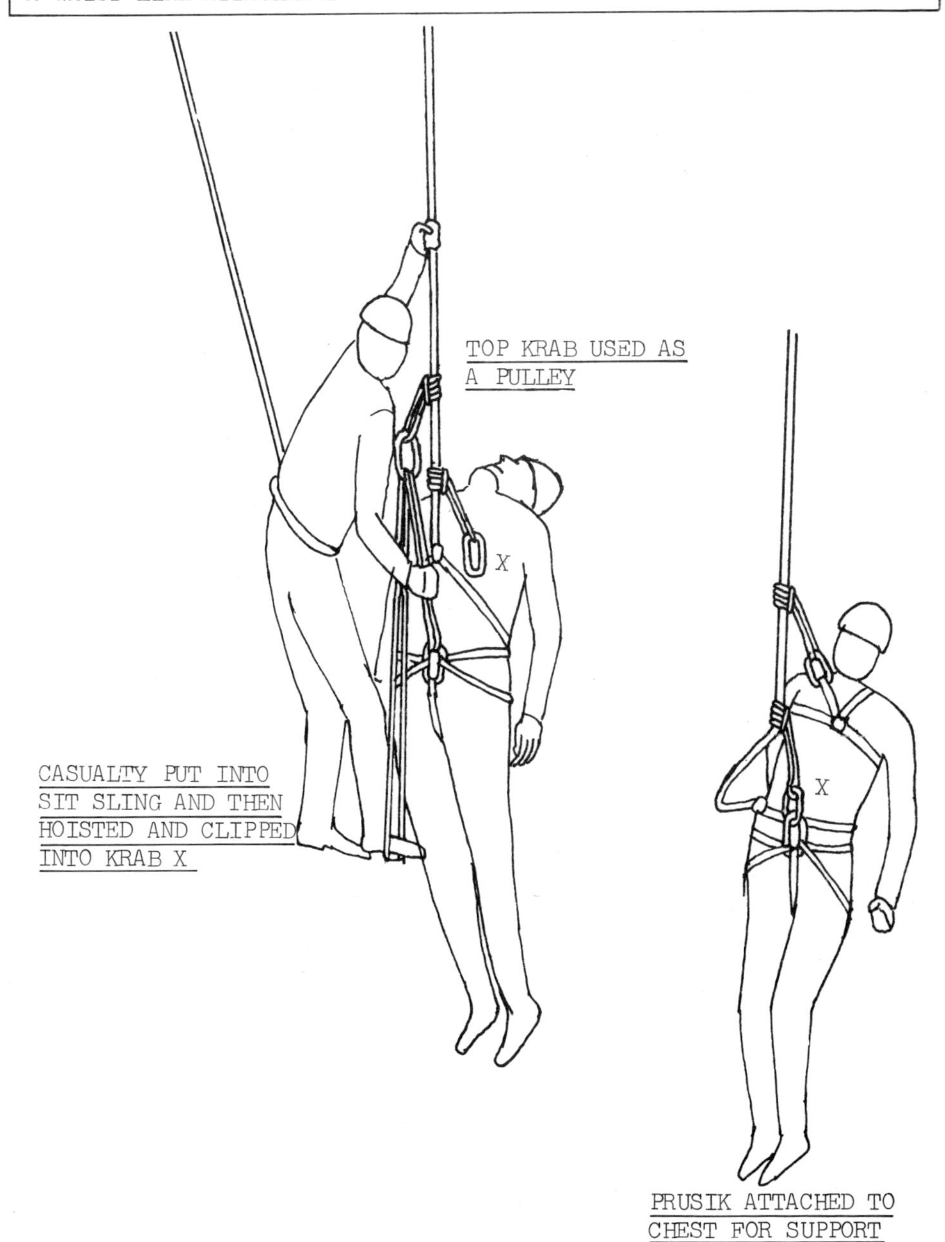

Tying off a Belay Rope under Load 

In the event of a fall in which there are no runners or the runners fail,the climber could face a situation where he needs to tie off the belay rope whilst it is directly under load. First he should wrap the inactive rope around his leg and stand on the end,thus securing the rope and releasing both hands. Then he attaches a prusik loop to the live rope and clips it back to the karabiner on the belay sling. If he cannot reach this he can clip back into the waistline karabiner (as long as the waistline karabiner does not fasten a belay belt). The prusik is pushed forward and the inactive rope released to transfer the weight to the prusik. The inactive rope is then tied in a figure of eight and clipped into the belay karabiner. The climber can now undo his waistline or belay belt and release himself from the belay. He is now free to render assistance or to go for help.

TYING OFF A BELAY ROPE UNDER LOAD

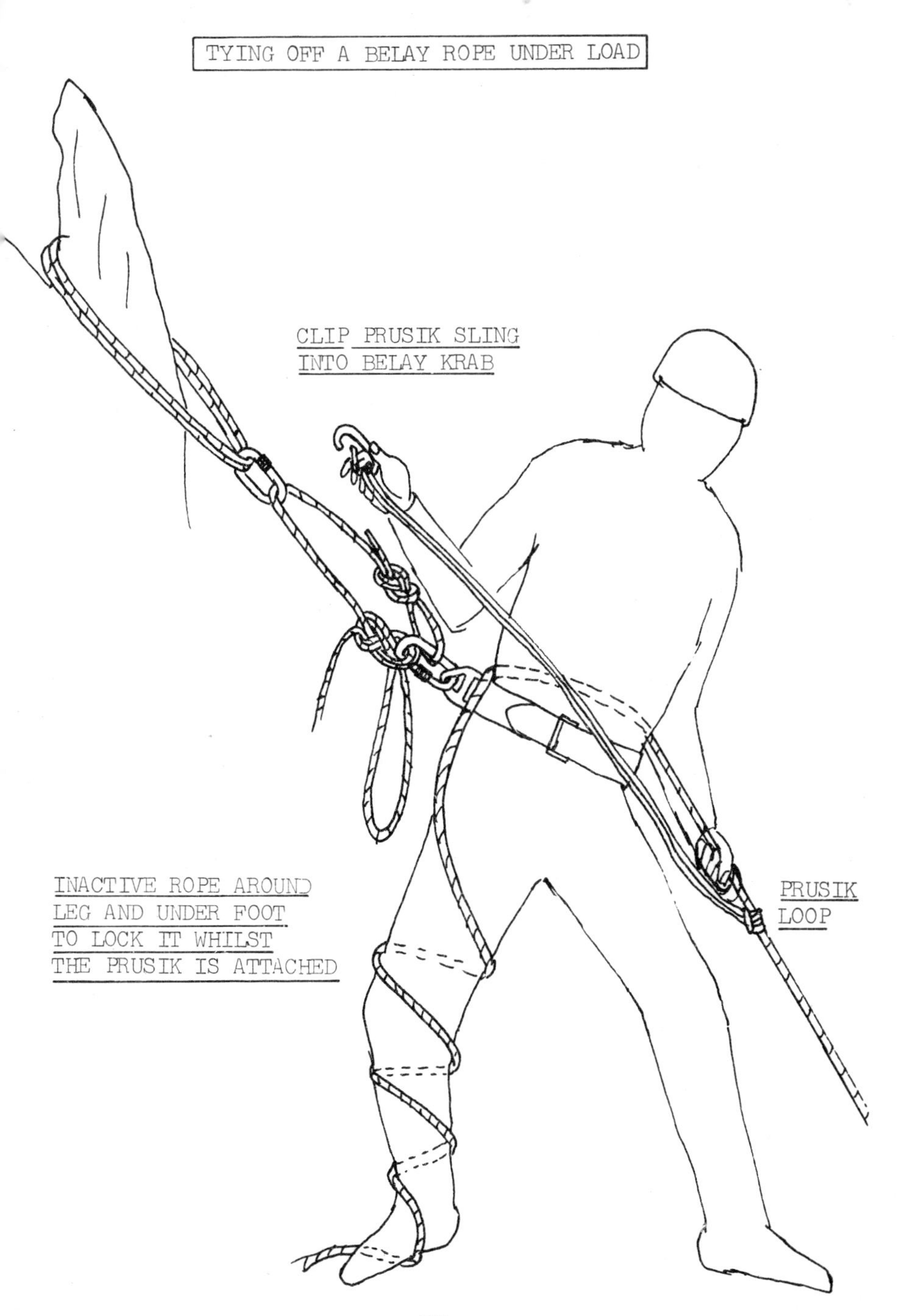

CHAPTER IV.

KARABINER BRAKES AND FRICTION DEVICES

LOWERING

CHAPTER IV.

KARABINER BRAKES AND FRICTION DEVICES. LOWERING.

Friction Devices

The application of friction devices is widespread in mountaineering - they are used for lowering, abseiling and in some instances, belaying. They may be divided into two categories - purpose built and improvised.

Purpose Built

These are specialised pieces of equipment, expensive enough to merit due consideration before purchase. Unless one contemplates a great deal of abseiling or lowering it is probably just as well to use the improvised methods available. There are, at the moment, four types of descenders on the market. The Figure of Eight, the Peck, Pierre Allain and the Fammu.

(i) The large Figure of Eight is the most foolproof and safest of the descenders. There is sufficient metal to dissipate heat, it is easy to assemble and operate, and it provides sufficient friction braking for a comfortable descent. A stretcher and barrow boy can easily be lowered on three of these. It is possible to lock the Figure of Eight by jamming the control rope across the top, or by tying off with a bight of rope in a half-hitch, or wrapping the control (lower) rope around the thigh. This is especially useful in cliff rescue situations. The thin wire Figure of Eight should not be used, as it may easily unclip from a karabiner. Care should be taken to keep clothing away from descenders as shirts or anoraks can be pulled in and jam the rope.
(ii) The Fammu descender operates on the same principle as the Figure of Eight and has the added advantage of separating the ropes as they pass through, thus facilitating an easy pull through the abseil rope.

(iii) The Peck descender is simply a long bar around which the rope is wound to provide friction. The degree of friction can be controlled by increasing or decreasing the number of turns around the bar. At the top the bar is hooked to prevent the release of the rope, however, there is a danger of the rope coming off if the load is released.
(iv) The Pierre Allain is a rather fragile looking descender which is also prone to release from the rope if it is unloaded.

DESCENDERS

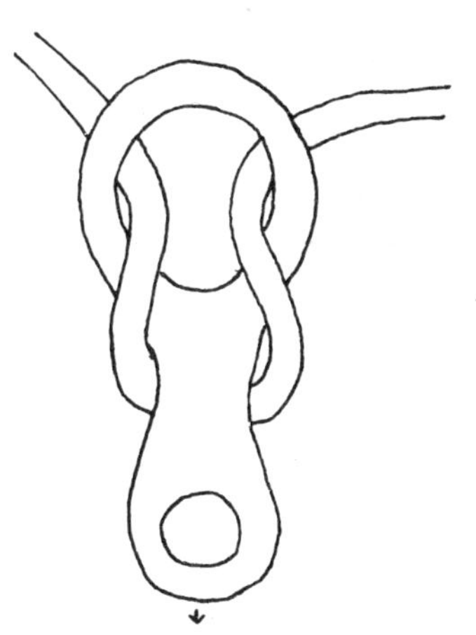

(i) FIGURE OF EIGHT

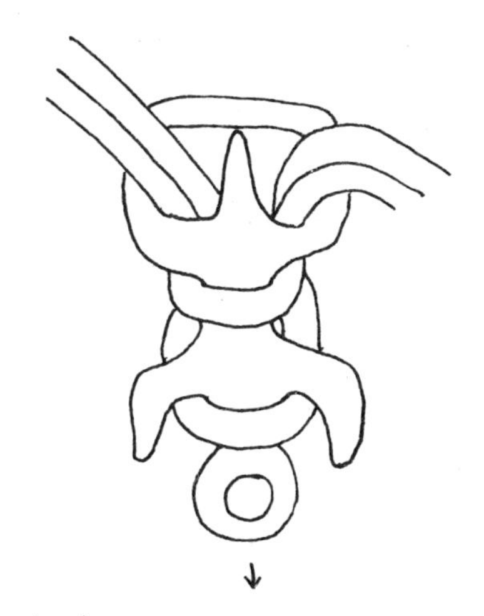

(ii) FAMMU

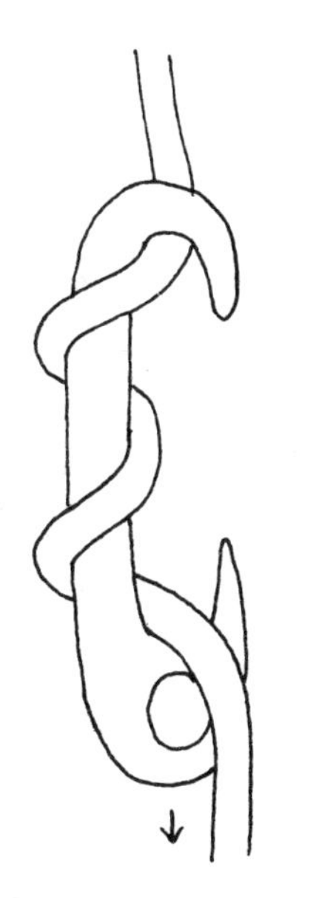

(iii) PECK

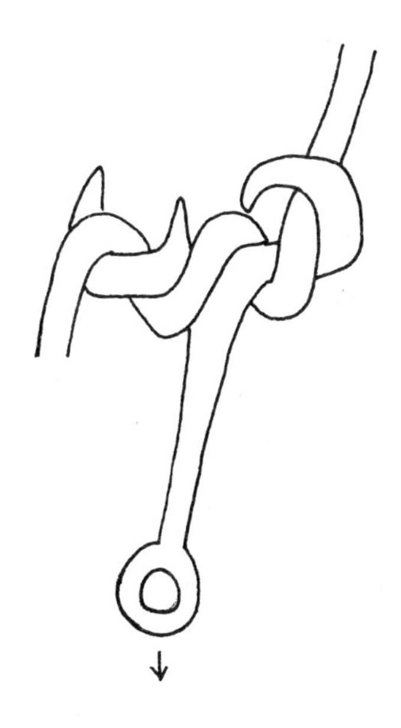

(iv) PIERRE ALLAIN

Friction Hitches

(i) Italian or Munter Hitch

This simple friction knot is a useful belaying method on kernmantel rope and may be used direct onto the anchor or on the belayer as with the Sticht plate. To assemble, clip the rope through the karabiner, then take a loop on the load rope side, twist once and clip into the karabiner. The friction is so effective that a fall can be arrested by holding the free rope with a gloved hand. It must not be used on hawser laid rope.

(ii) Simple Twist on Karabiner

The twist of rope around the karabiner is a simple friction device, less effective than the Italian hitch. On occasion, the rope may cross over itself in the Karabiner and cause some difficulty in control. Like the Italian hitch it should only be used with kernmantel ropes as it tends to kink hawser laid.

(iii) Sticht Belay Plate

The Sticht belay plate is simply a bar with a slot, through which a loop of the climbing rope is fed and clipped into a karabiner. The karabiner may be attached directly to the belayer's anchor, or to the belayer's chest harness, or waist line, if he is secure. The rope is fed through the plate with gloved hands and a fall is arrested by simply moving the control rope away from the karabiner, causing the rope to run in an S shape through the system. There are small holes in each corner of the plate so it may be laced up to the karabiner with line, to prevent it sliding too far down the rope. Two types of plate are manufactured - a single for 11mm rope and a double for 9mm rope. Although designed by Fritz Sticht as a belay device, the plate may be used for abseiling or lowering.

FRICTION HITCHES

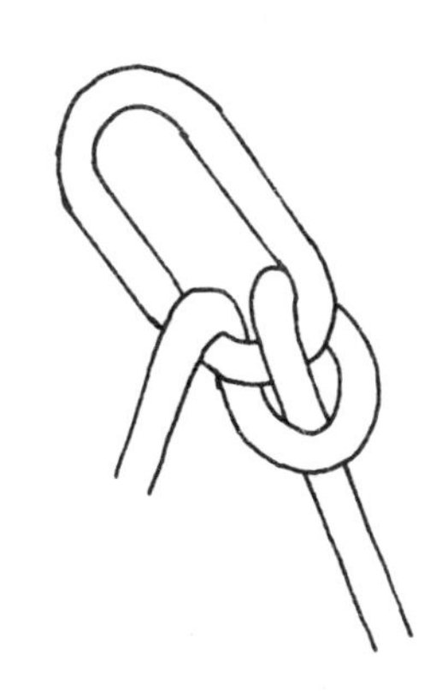

(i) ITALIAN HITCH

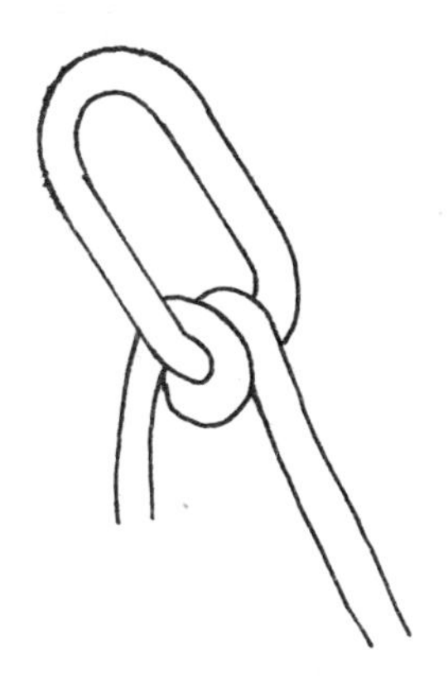

(ii) SIMPLE TWIST AROUND A KARABINER

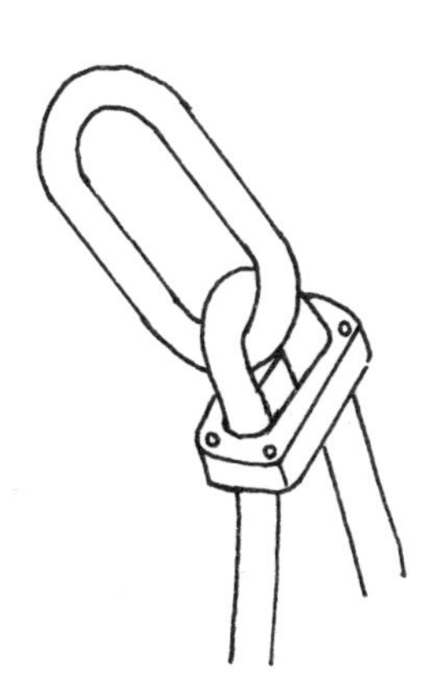

(iii) STICHT BELAY PLATE

Karabiner Brakes

The karabiner brake is a very useful improvised device wherever any lowering or abseiling is needed. There are many friction devices or descenders on the market, but they are specialized equipment and are carried by few, whereas karabiners are multi-purpose and are carried by many.

To assemble the brake, one karabiner is clipped across the other with the rope running through and over the transverse bar. Once learnt, it is simple to use and saves wear and tear on clothing and expenditure of energy. The brake operated correctly gives a smooth lower, superior to the waist belay lowers. Its applications are many, especially on cliff rescue, e.g. the lowering of stretchers, tragsitzs, oneself with a casualty, people who will not, or cannot, abseil and also, of course, abseiling.

As a method of abseiling it has much to recommend it; control and locking are simple and there is no strain on the body. The karabiner brake moves down the rope, consequently it must be inverted in order that the control rope is fed from below. The control rope is held on the back bar side of the karabiner running parallel to the rope, and is passed under the thigh and held on the right hand. If the person wishes to stop, the rope may be wrapped around the thigh, thus locking the brake. This leaves the hands free to deal with emergency situations, e.g. freeing jammed ropes, untangling kinks, administering aid to a person on a cliff, undertaking a difficult pendulum, removing gear, etc.

Assembled Karabiner Brake

1. The load rope is nearest you when facing the brake.
2. The gate of the 1st karabiner points in an anti-clockwise direction.
3. The rope tightens both screw gates as it passes.
4. The control rope is held on the backbar side of the first karabiner, i.e. the karabiner parallel with the rope.
5. The gate of the first karabiner points to the belay.

If these are correct, the brake is correct.

Operation of Karabiner Brakes

1. A fast lower may result in over heating of the karabiner due to friction; the lower should be steady and smooth with a double brake fitted if the load is heavy.

2. Check the rope for kinks or knots as these could jam the brake. The rope should be fed into the brake to avoid this happening. If there is no danger of the rope snagging it may be left hanging over the cliff.

3. Remember the brake is a one way system; it cannot reverse without releasing the load and feeding back the rope by hand.

4. The belay is directly loaded, therefore, reduce the shock loading and the vibration by attaching the karabiner brake with a sling. Always have a karabiner clipped on the belay side of the brake separating it from the sling.

5. The load on the brake should be constant as jerking and unloading could result in the braking karabiner (transverse to the rope) slipping down and fouling the brake.

ASSEMBLY OF KARABINER BRAKE WITH CONTROL ROPE ABOVE

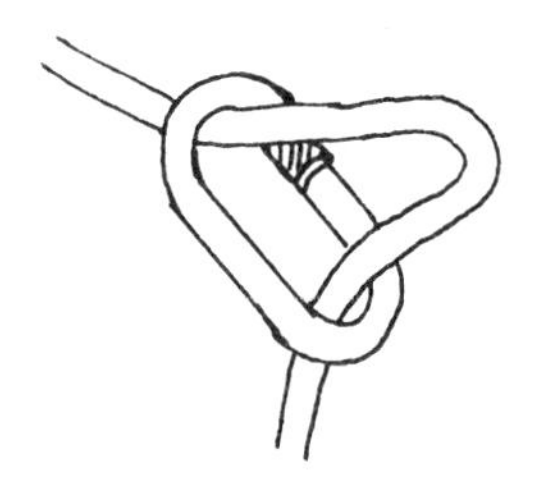

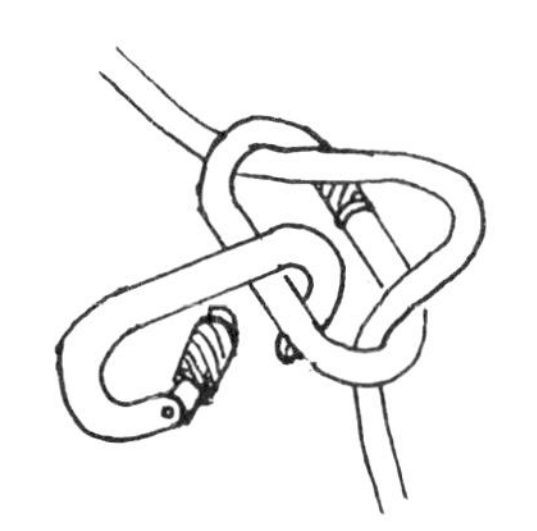

(i) HOLD KRAB IN RIGHT HAND WITH THE GATE POINTING UP AND ANTI CLOCKWISE. PUSH A LOOP OF ROPE UP FROM BELOW THROUGH THE KRAB. KEEP THE LOAD ROPE NEAREST YOU.

(ii) HOLD THE SECOND KRAB IN LEFT HAND IN THE SAME POSITION AS THE FIRST AND CLIP INTO THE BACK BAR OF THE KRAB FROM ABOVE.

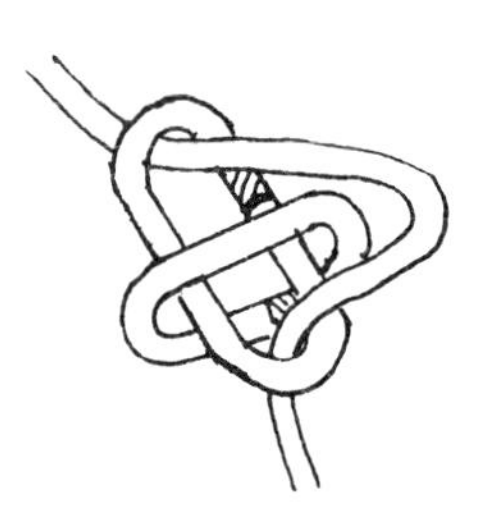

(iii) NOW CLIP THE SECOND KRAB INTO OTHER SIDE OF KRAB OVER THE GATE

ASSEMBLY OF KARABINER BRAKE WITH CONTROL ROPE BELOW

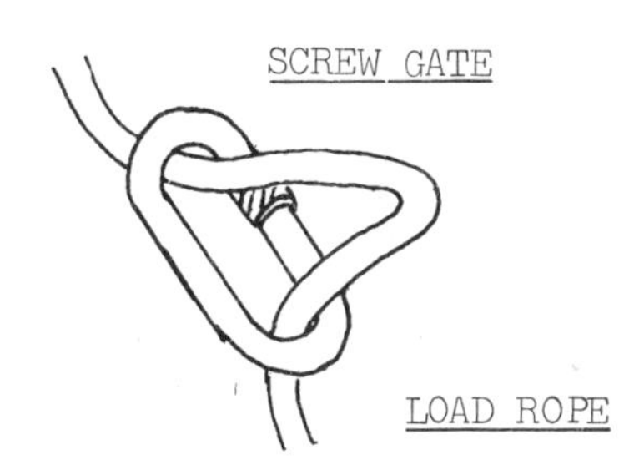

(i) HOLD THE KRAB IN RIGHT HAND WITH THE GATE POINTING UP AND ANTI CLOCKWISE. PUSH A LOOP OF ROPE UP FROM BELOW THROUGH THE KRAB. KEEP THE LOAD ROPE NEAREST YOU.

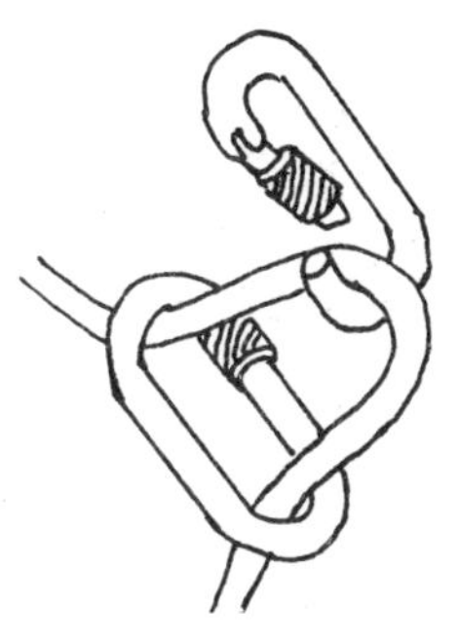

(ii) HOLD THE SECOND KRAB WITH YOUR LEFT HAND IN THE SAME POSITION AS THE FIRST AND CLIP INTO THE LOOP OF ROPE FROM ABOVE.

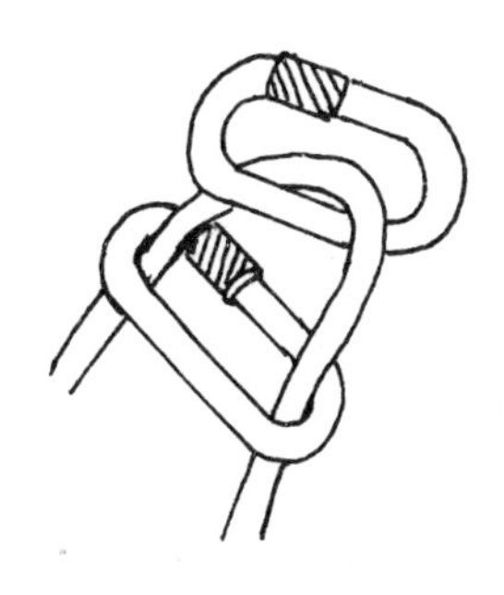

(iii) TURN THE SECOND KRAB GATE UPPERMOST.

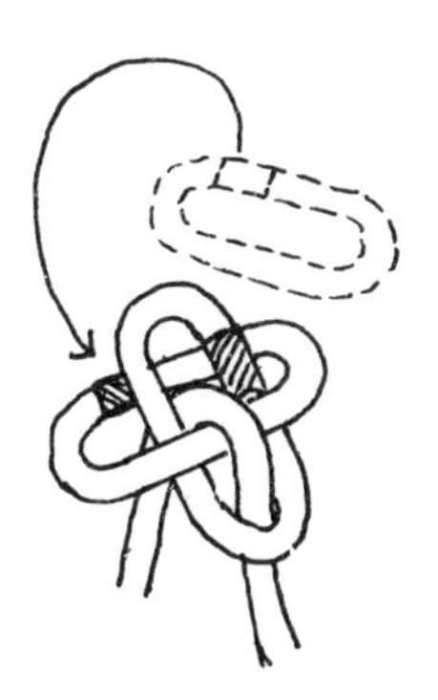

(iv) TWIST THE SECOND KRAB BACK DROPPING ITS GATE BEHIND THE FIRST KRAB.

KARABINER BRAKES

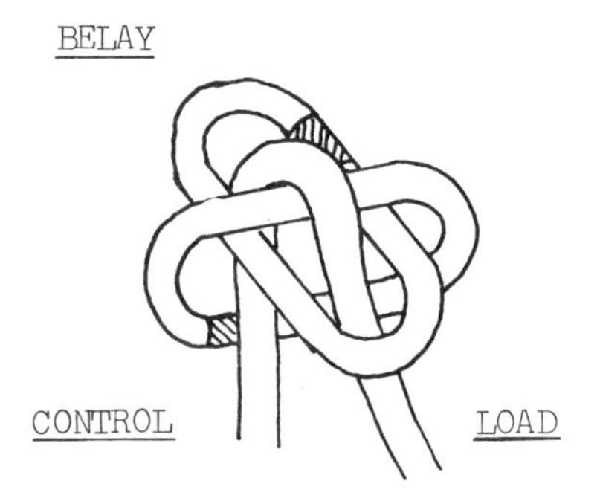

(i) CONTROL ROPE BELOW

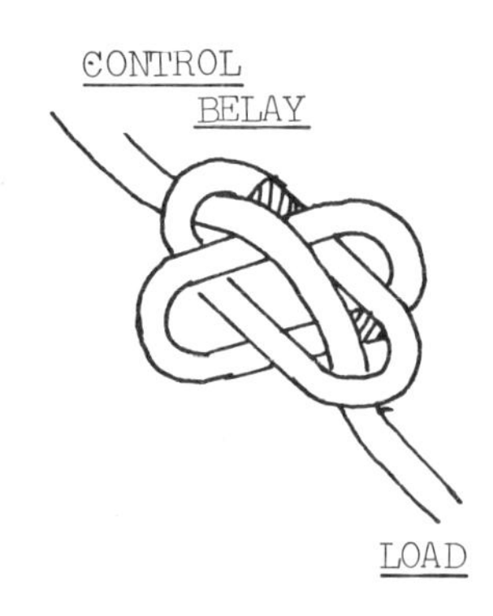

(ii) CONTROL ROPE ABOVE

TYING OFF A KRAB BRAKE

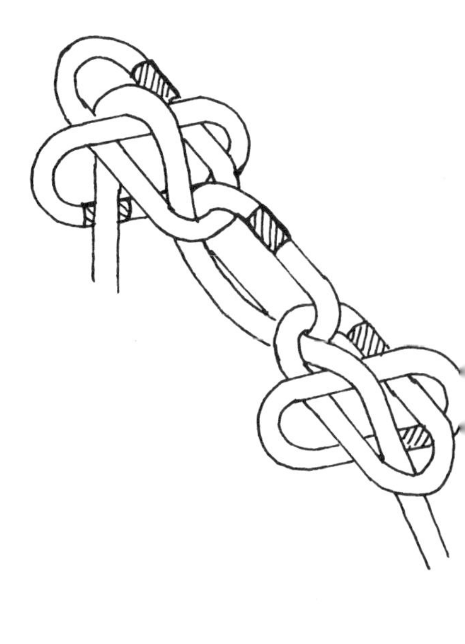

DOUBLE KARABINER BRAKE

6. It is possible to increase friction and stop the lower by bringing the control rope forward across the brake. A prusik knot may be tied below the brake on the load rope to give an independent locking system. The other end of the prusik sling should be secured by a knot which can be released under tension e.g. Mariner Knot.

7. When possible the brake operator should feed the rope from a waist belay and should be belayed separately. It is possible, however, to feed hand over hand or even one handed, and with practice one man can operate two brakes. Gloves should be worn.

8. A brake may be locked and tied off with a bight of rope in a half hitch which can be released under load by pulling the free end.

Double Karabiner Brake

When a heavy load is being lowered and more friction is required a double karabiner brake can be used. This is operated and tied off exactly the same as a single brake.

Improvised Friction Brakes

There are several improvised friction brakes which can be used when karabiners are in short supply - the brake bar (fig.i) from the crossed karabiner may be replaced by the shaft of a peg hammer (fig.ii) or by an angle piton clipped into a karabiner and placed across (fig.iv). Either of these methods are as efficient as the slide on, brake bar which can be bought for this purpose.

Lowering the Tragsitz

1. By a climber above, through a karabiner brake.
2. By the carry man himself lowering through a karabiner brake anchored above.
3. By the carry man himself abseiling with the casualty on a karabiner brake. In this instance the doubled abseil rope could either be passed under the leg for greater friction or split and held apart, one in each hand. The latter possibly gives greater control of the abseil.

Karabiner Brake Made With Non Screw Gate Karabiners

In certain circumstances screw gate karabiners may not be available and non screw gate karabiners may have to be used. The safest brake to use is made with four non screw gate karabiners. Superimpose two karabiners with back bars covering the gates to prevent the rope slipping out. Now assemble the brake in the normal way clipping one karabiner in from one side and one in from the other. This is a perfectly safe brake for abseiling and lowering if the normal operating instructions are followed.(Fig.iii)

IMPROVISED FRICTION BRAKES

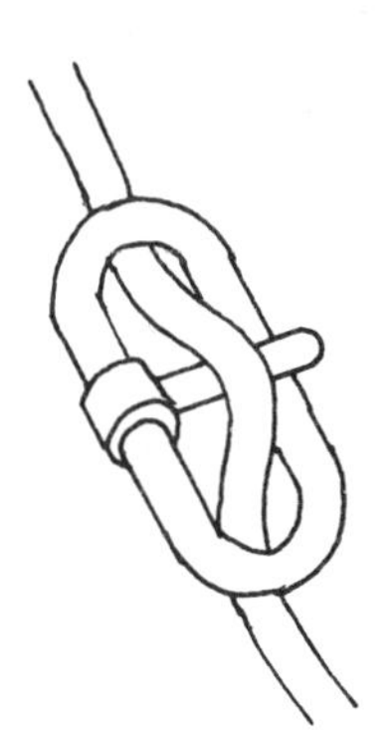

(i) KARABINER BRAKE BAR.

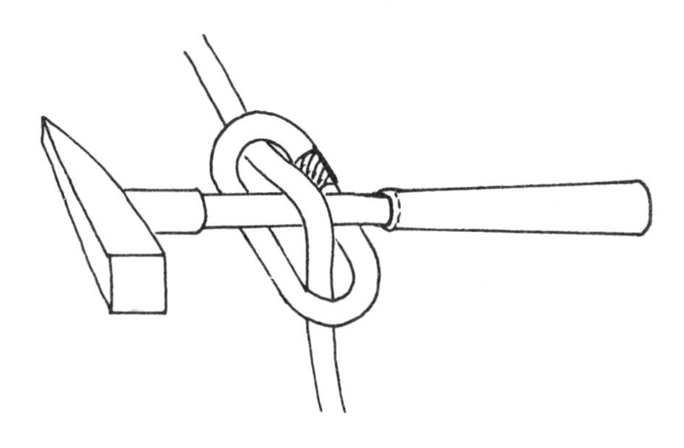

(ii) HAMMER SHAFT AND KRAB.

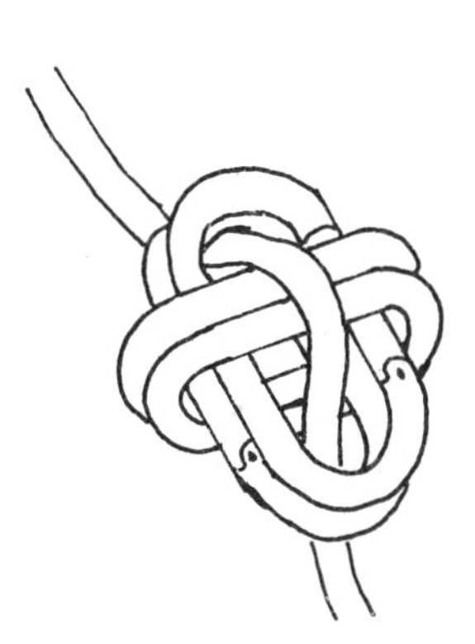

(iii) KARABINER BRAKE MADE WITH NON SCREW GATE KRABS BACK TO BACK.

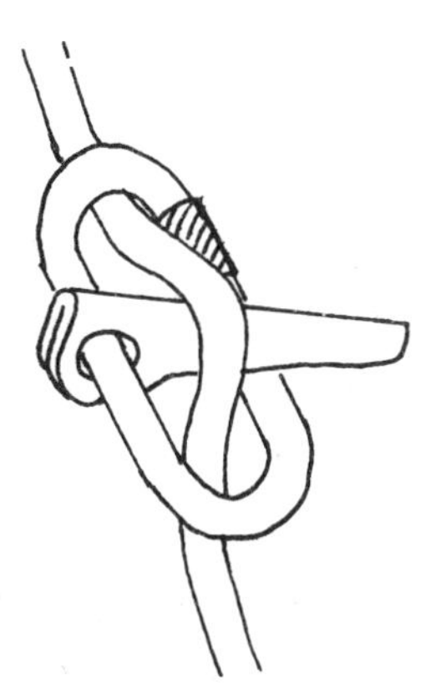

(iv) ANGLE PITON USED AS BRAKE BAR.

PASSING A KNOT THROUGH A KARABINER BRAKE

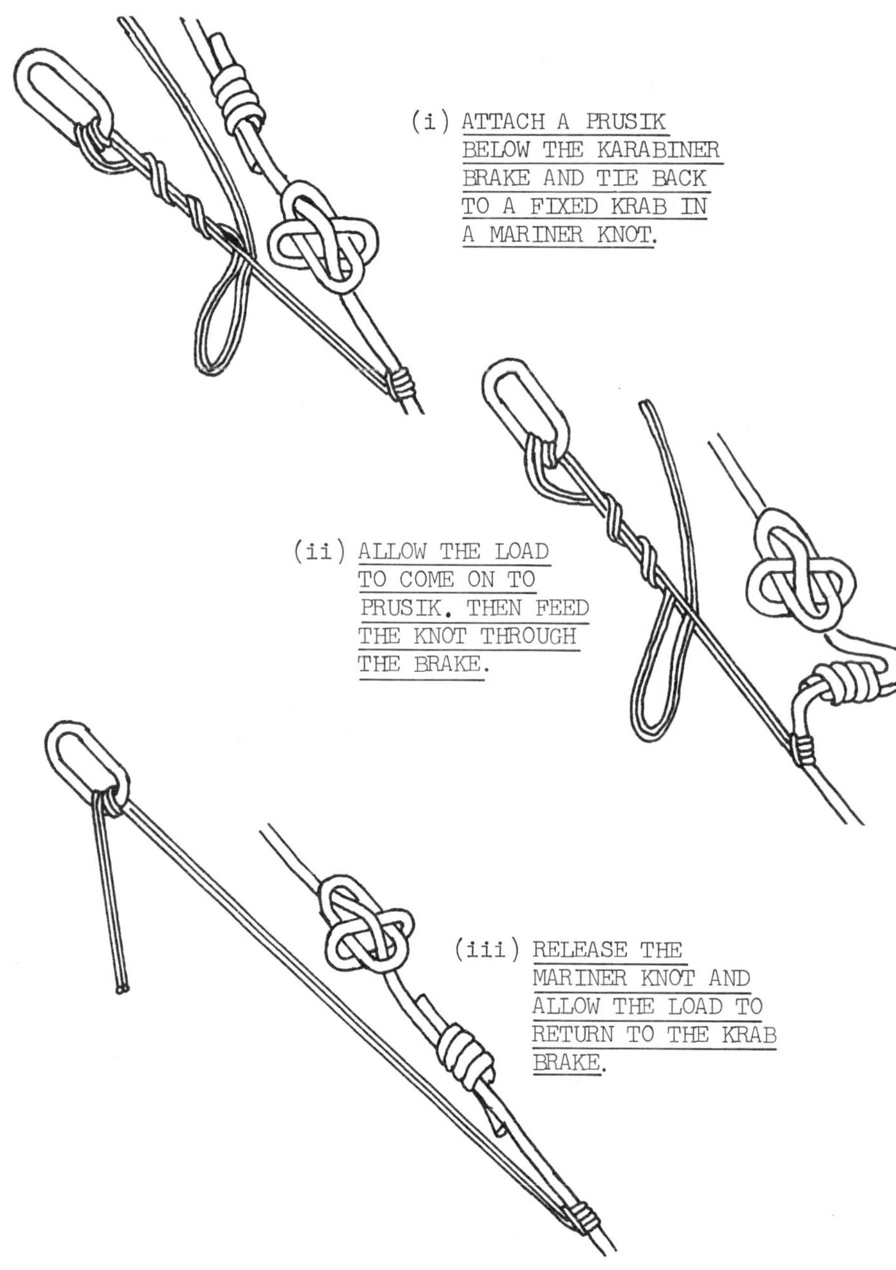

CHAPTER V.

IMPROVISED STRETCHERS AND CARRIES

CHAPTER V.

IMPROVISED STRETCHERS AND CARRIES

Improvised Carries

There is always a liklihood of the minor mishap when hill-walking or climbing, which can be handled by a strong and competent party without recourse to outside assistance. In these minor accident situations a knowledge of improvised carrying techniques is invaluable. When the casualty is light and small e.g. a child, then very often a one man carry is sufficient. The casualty can be carried pick-a-back, or in a split rope carry, two sling pole carry, or a rucksack carry. The split rope carry is effected by dividing a coil of rope into two sections and placing the casualties' legs into the separate coils. The coils are put on like rucksack straps and take the weight of the casualty on the carrier's shoulders. The split sling carry is simply two slings worn bandolier fashion with a pole (ski stick-ice axe-tent pole) passed through the back of the carrier and well padded. The casualty is carried pick-a-back with his legs resting on the pole. The rucksack may be used in a variety of ways - one method is to pad the bottom of the empty sack and lengthen the straps, the casualty sits on the padding and places his legs through the straps of the rucksack which is worn in the usual way by the carrier.

A carry which is useful for short distances where it is necessary to keep the person's head down is the fireman's lift.

All the one man carries have limited use as the carrier must be strong and the casualty light. They are only effective as short distance emergency carries.

The two man rope carries are less strenuous than one man carries but they can be more awkward on narrow tracks and over difficult ground. A rope coil can be split and the separate

IMPROVISED CARRIES

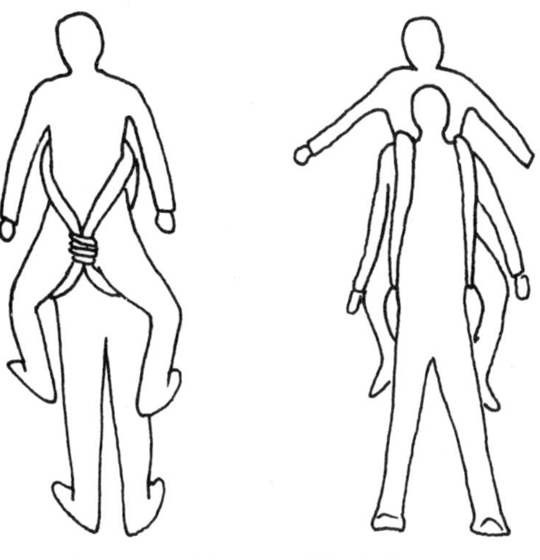

ONE MAN SPLIT ROPE CARRY

CROSSED SLINGS
AND POLE CARRY

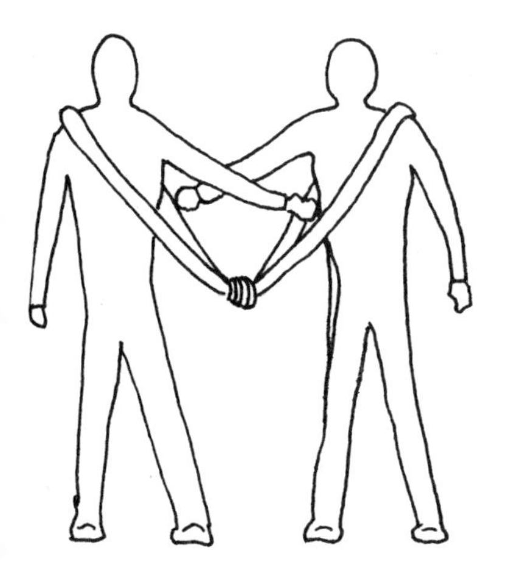

TWO MAN SPLIT ROPE CARRY

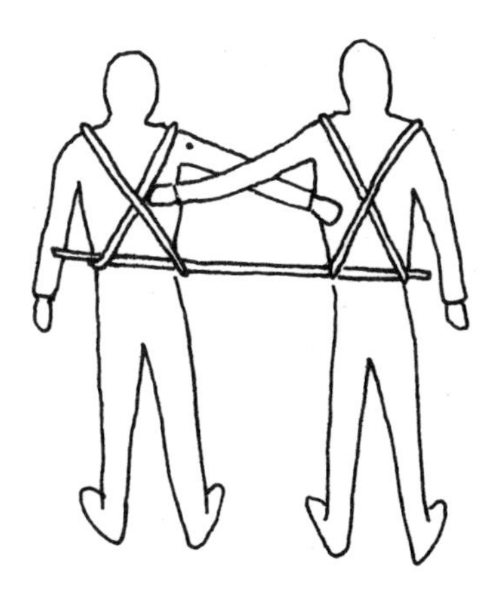

TWO MAN SLING AND POLE CARRY

coils carried bandolier fashion by two people standing side by side, the whipping on the rope providing the seat. The carriers link arms behind the casualty to provide a back rest. A two man pole can be constructed by passing a pole through crossed slings or rucksack straps worn by two people. The pole should be well padded for the comfort of the casualty.

Improvised Stretchers

Pigott Rope Stretcher -

The most common improvised stretcher known today is the Pigott Rope stretcher. It consists of a length of No.2 rope usually tied off in a series of loops with the overhand knot. The spare rope runs down joining the ends of the loops to form the side of the stretcher. Instead of using the old method of joining the loops by doubling the ends and laboriously threading the rope through, a sheet bend may be tied. In order to facilitate tying the knot, hold the rope in coils. The cross loops can be reinforced by running the spare rope down the centre of the stretcher and tying to each one with an overhand knot. The stretcher should then be turned over so that the knots do not dig into the casualty's back. In any event the rope stretcher should be well padded for the casualty's comfort. It is possible for an experienced person to construct a Pigott using this method in less than fifteen minutes.

IMPROVED PIGOTT STRETCHER

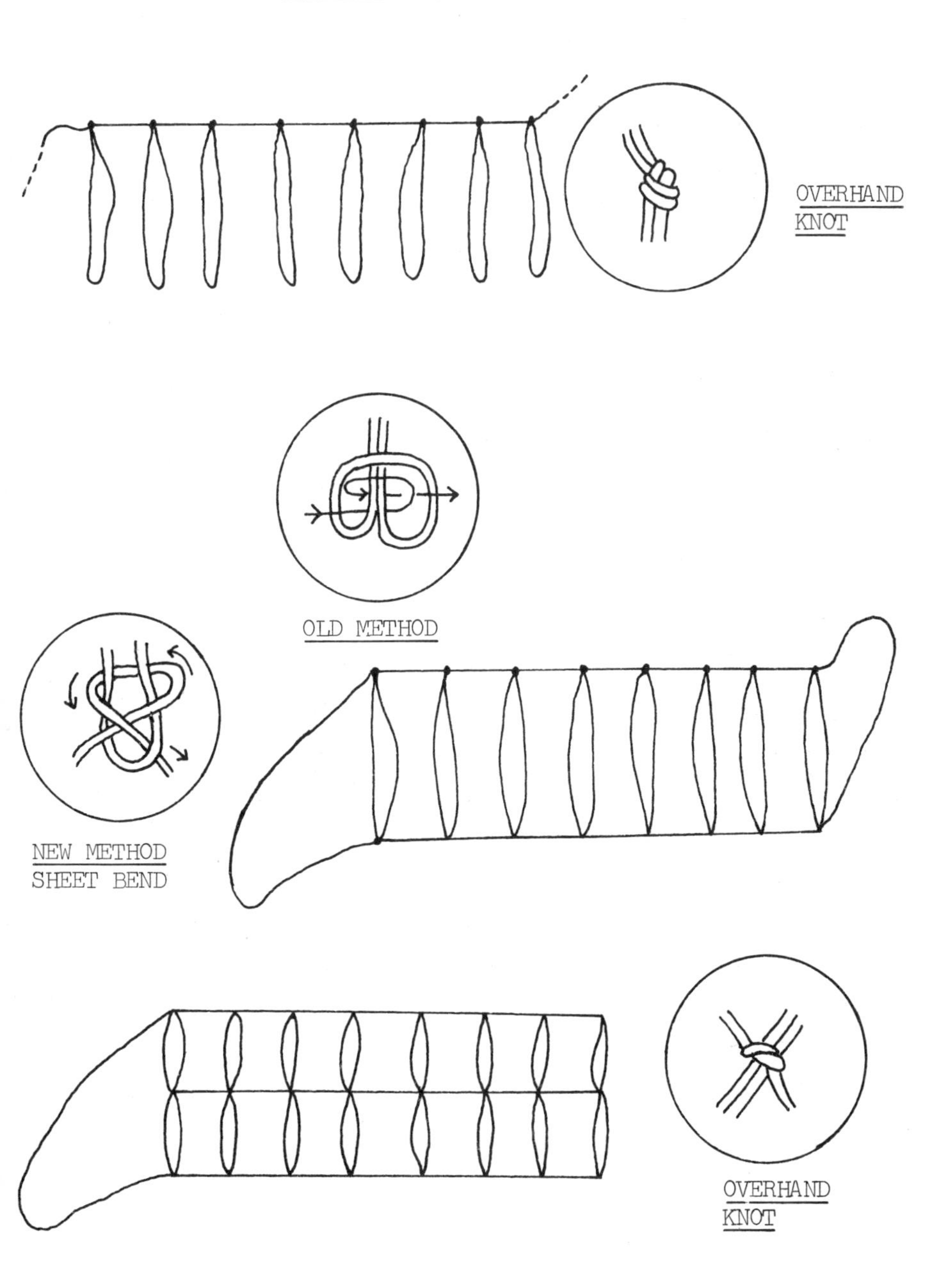

The Alpine Basket -

The Alpine rope basket is an even quicker way of constructing an emergency stretcher although initially designed as a lowering cradle in improvised cliff rescues. There are three methods of construction. (i) A loop for the feet is tied in the end of the rope which is then laid down in a series of S shaped loops on the ground. The patient is placed on the loops which are laced through one another from the feet to the chest leaving the arms outside. The top is tied off as a chest harness crossed at the back and the spare rope is used to provide carrying handles. (ii) The next method is to tie a bowline on the bight to give two loops which are used as a chest harness, the casualty is then laced on the normal manner and tied off at the feet. It is important that the first loops be threaded through the top of the chest tie. This method is quicker and easier than the Pigott. (iii) The third method is - lay down a series of loops much longer than in methods one and two and to offset the casualty on the loops. The long loop is then tied off on the opposite short loop in a sheet bend and the long bight can then be used as a carrying handle.

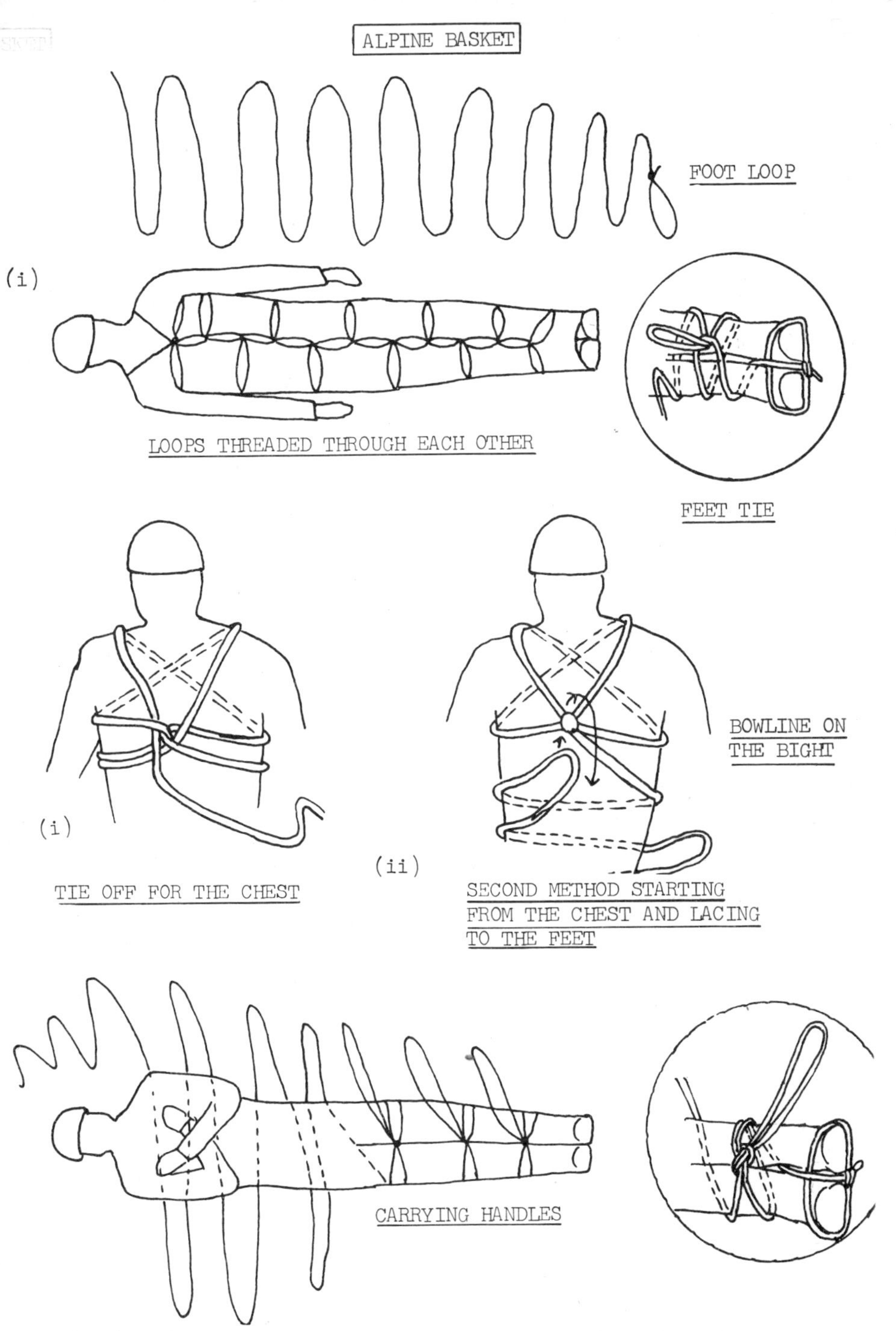
ALPINE BASKET
FOOT LOOP
(i)
LOOPS THREADED THROUGH EACH OTHER
FEET TIE
BOWLINE ON
THE BIGHT
(i)
TIE OFF FOR THE CHEST
(ii)
SECOND METHOD STARTING
FROM THE CHEST AND LACING
TO THE FEET
CARRYING HANDLES
(iii) THIRD METHOD TIE OFF LONGER LOOPS WITH A SHEET BEND

Both the Pigott and the rope basket lack rigidity and are consequently difficult to carry and they cannot be used for spinal injuries. They may be improved by adding rigidity in the form of crossed ice axes lashed together and well padded. Pack frames may be used to reinforce the stretcher or can be lashed and splinted together to form a rigid carrying platform. If there are some long poles available, e.g. tent poles, skis, a rope lacing stretcher can be constructed. The knots on the stretcher poles may be overhand on the bight or clove hitches. Transverse rigidity may be obtained by lashing cross members at the head and foot of the stretcher. It is possible to use two anoraks with poles through the sleeves to make a stretcher when no rope is available.

There are of course many improvisations possible, depending on the materials available at the time, and there is little doubt that quite long carries can be undertaken with well built, rigid, improvised stretchers. Rope stretchers and individual carrying methods can only be used for short carries. Always remember the limitations as well as the advantages of the improvised carrying techniques when you are considering using them.

IMPROVISED STRETCHERS

OVERHAND KNOT

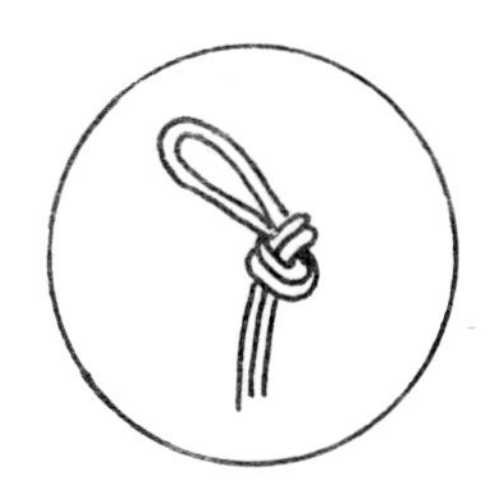

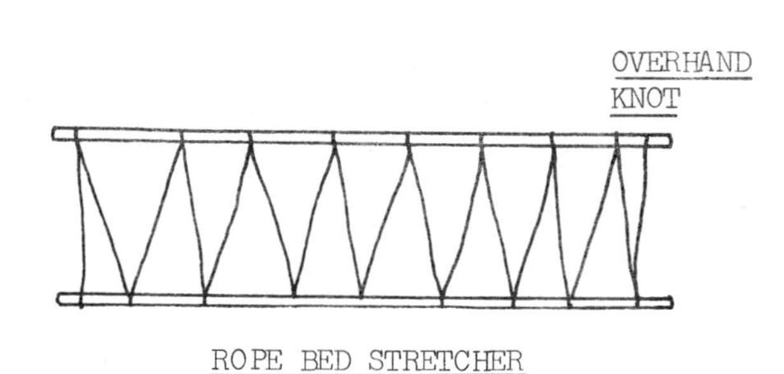

ROPE BED STRETCHER

CLOVE HITCH

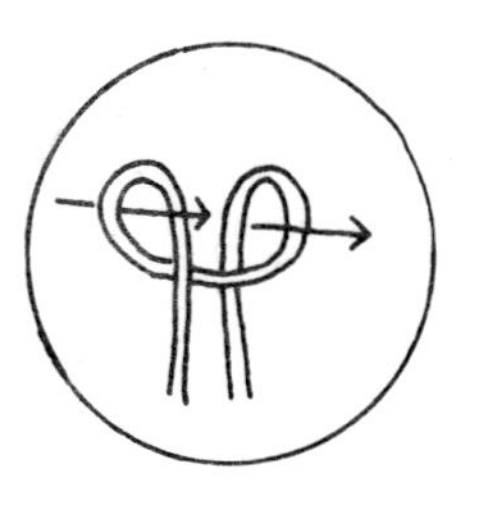

POLES

STRETCHER MADE FROM TWO ANORAKS

POLE

CASUALTY'S WEIGHT HOLDS FOLDED GROUND SHEET IN POSITION

STRETCHER MADE FROM GROUND SHEET

CHAPTER VI.

BELAYING

CHAPTER VI.

BELAYING

Tying to the Belay

The climbing rope is tied in a figure of eight knot on the bight at the end and clipped to the waistbelt by a screw gate karabiner. Tie the loose end of the rope with an overhand knot close to the first knot. To secure oneself to a belay pass the rope round the anchor or clip into a karabiner as appropriate and tuck a bight of the free rope through the waistline karabiner and tie off on itself with a figure of eight or two half hitches. Ensure there is at least an 18 inch loop left after the belay knot has been tied as a short loop may be pulled through the knot under load.

The Belay

Each stance and belay is a new situation which the climber must examine and use to the best mechanical advantage. Few are perfect, but with the application of a few basic rules, they can be made secure.

The Position of the Belay Relative to the Stance

The belayer should always be below his belay as he may be pulled down on a low belay point. If there are only low belays available the belayer should sit down. Indeed, many people advise sitting down whenever taking a waist belay and there is much to recommend it, e.g. greater stability, no likelihood of buckling at the legs, comfort.

Length of Belay

Long belays should be used with care as they are liable to sideways instability and to stretching. Always keep back from the edge of the stance and make an allowance for belay stretch.

When you arrive at the stance select your belays - two abou 3 feet apart for stability. Belay onto one and adjust the bight of tied off rope so it clips into the second belay. This avoids tying back to the waistline karabiner twice. Take up a stance in such a position that the tension is equally divided between the belays and both are tight. Check that the belay and stance are in line with the anticipated strain. The whole leg, including the hip on the active rope side, should be advanced 45 degrees to anticipate the turning force exerted when the rope tightens under load. The feet should be apart providing a triangle of stabilit and the knees should be slightly flexed. Gloves which protect the wrist, as well as the hands should be worn. The inactive rope should be twisted once around the arm on the inactive side t give extra friction. Once the belayer is satisfied he should as himself what would happen if the rope is pulled hard. This is his final test before entering into communication with his climbi partner.

The climbing calls are one of the most misused, misunderstoo communication systems in operation. The call by the leader "taking in" means that the leader is belayed and is taking in the rope hand over hand. It does not mean that the second can undo his belay. When the rope comes tight on the second the call "that's me" indicates to both climbers that the rope is not snagged anywhere and the system is live. The leader then adopts the belay position and belays the second. The call "climb when you are ready" means that the leader is belaying the second and the latter can now undo his belay. The second shouts "climbing" to indicate he is ready to climb, the leader replies "o.k." to signify he is taking in. It is essential to adhere to this system if adequate safety is to be maintained. The calls "take in", "more rope", "below", "runner on", "runner off" are self explanatory. All calls should be short and simple. Extended long distance conversations can be avoided by careful briefing, demonstration, sensible runner placement and good route selection.

Holding a Fall

To hold a fall, bring both arms across the front of the body, thus increasing the friction between the body and the rope. The rope will run and no attempt should be made to snatch hold it, - a gradual arrest is better for the belayer and the belayed. The strain of holding a direct leader fall is considerable and every effort should be made to place a good runner as soon as you leave the belay stance. The main belay must be able to take an upward pull in these instances.

Lowering From a Waist Belay

(i) First, adopt the belay position.

a. Feet apart

b. Knees flexed

c. Belay tight and in line with direction of anticipated strain

d. Foot and body advanced 45 degrees on live rope side.

e. Twist rope around arm on inactive side.

(ii) Second, bring arms across the front of the body as if to hold a fall and allow the weight to come on the rope. Hold and then release slowly by opening arms and easing grip. Avoid a jerky lower by allowing the weight to run slowly of its own accord.

This method places considerable strain on the belayer and his back should be adequately padded to minimise the discomfort. Friction devices afford an easier lower but they place a direct load on the belay and should not be used when belays are suspect. In the absence of adequate anchors waist belay lowers may be used.

Anchor Points

The most important single factor in any rescue situation is the provision of sound anchor, or belay points. They may be divided into natural belays and artificial belays. Natural belays are rock spikes, natural chockstones jammed in cracks, natural threads and trees. They should always be tested and loose chocks and spikes avoided. Large detached boulders and small trees should be regarded with suspicion, as should any tree which shows signs of decay. When necessary always use another belay to back up the one you have selected, and never hesitate to use artificial belays if the need arises. The selection and choice of belays is really one of experience and one must examine fully any anchor point selected from all angles and aspects. Remember that thread and chockstone belays withstand a pull in any direction and are the safest belays. Small stones and boulders can be inserted into cracks to make belays and can be hammered home for security.

Artificial Belays

There are two types of artificial belays apart from bolts, the inserted metal chockstone and the piton. Metal chockstones on wire are available in a wide range of sizes and are very good belays as they are easily inserted. Again, experience is necessary in selecting cracks - flared cracks and cracks with parallel sides should be avoided, as should placed chockstones held by small rugosities. A well placed chockstone should be in a narrowing crack and should be able to withstand a horizontal pull as well as a downward pull, e.g. the walls of the crack should be closer together at the surface. Cracks in detached blocks should be avoided as they may be wedged apart under load. Always check the soundness of the rock with a piton hammer and avoid areas of rock with a dull hollow sound.

Pitons

There are two types of pitons; hard steel or chrome molybdenum pitons, which do not bend and hold by wedging in the placement cracks, and soft steel, which follow the line of the crack. Soft steel pitons are obsolete and should not be used if hard steel pitons are available. The hard steel pitons on the market are generally well designed, with heads which lie flush to the rock when hammered home and with gradual, rather than sharp tapers. There are various designs to cover a wide range of cracks, from very thin and hairline cracks, to cracks over 6 inches in width. The thinner pitons are designed for aid climbing only although the Hiten pitons have great holding power and have been used for main belays. The basic designs for the wider cracks are i. Leepers, which have a "Z" shaped profile and are placed in vertical cracks with the eye uppermost and in horizontal cracks with the eye down. ii. Angles, which have "V" shaped profiles and are placed with the eye down in horizontal cracks. Both types of pitons are placed so the edges bite into the side of the crack. The angles grade into bongs as they increase in size.

Placement of Pitons

When placing pitons always choose the crack which gives the best mechanical advantage, e.g. horizontal cracks sloping slightly downwards into the rock. Avoid blind cracks, shattered areas, downward sloping cracks in roofs and overhangs, cracks which open out above and below the piton position. The correct piton to use is one which will enter two thirds of the way in without hammering. If it is too big, do not overdrive, but tie off with a sling in a clove hitch. Always sling the piton if there is any danger of the karabiner acting as a lever and make sure the gate of the karabiner is pointing down. If the pitons you have are too small

BELAYING ON ROCK

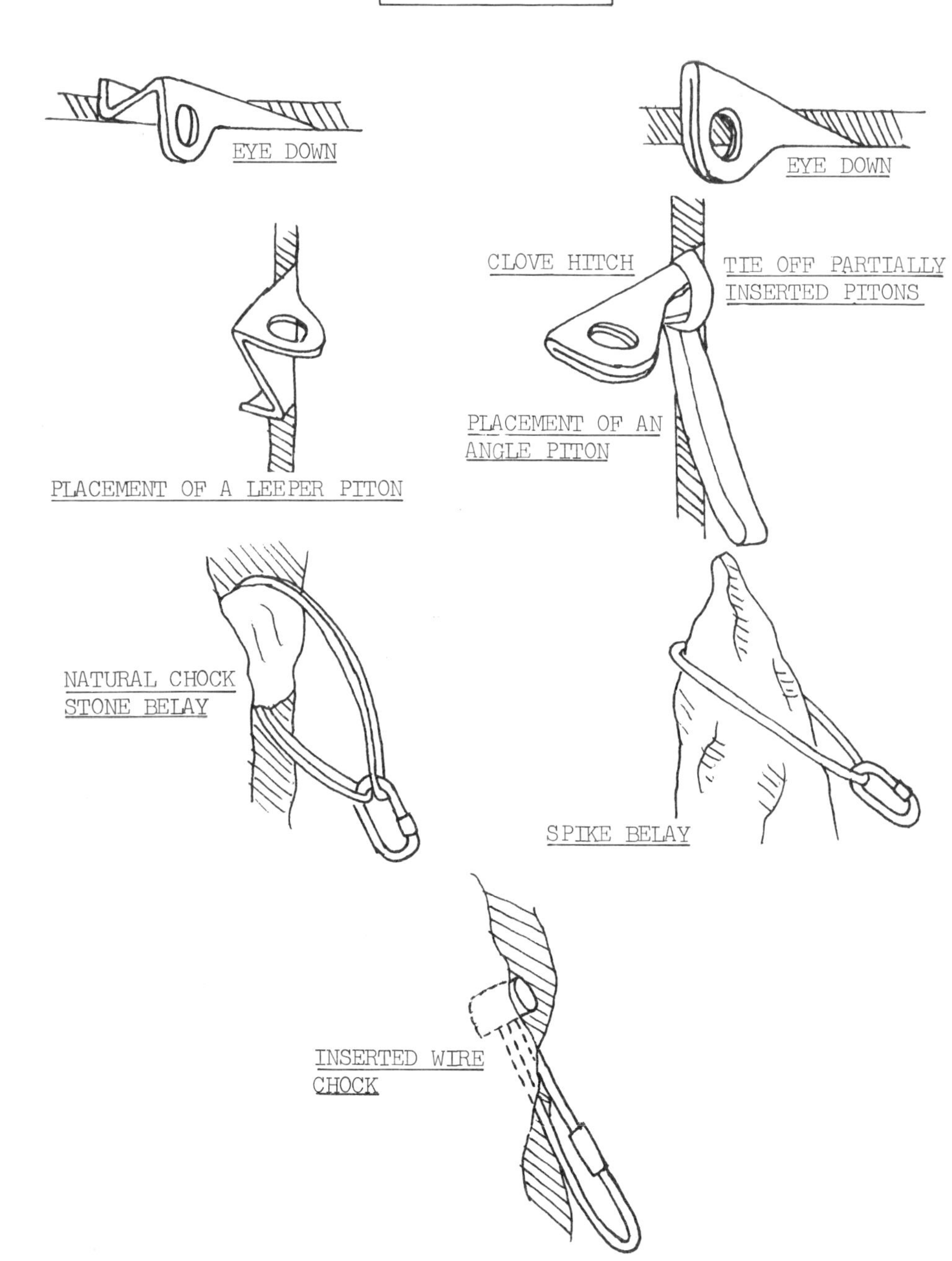

for the cracks available you may be able to stack them. Leepers are the best pegs to insert together and stack. Stacking is used mainly in aid climbing and should only be used in main belays when there is no alternative. In winter cracks are often choked with ice and pitons with channels, e.g. Leepers and angles are the most effective as the ice can be extruded via the channels as the piton is inserted.

Belaying On Snow and Ice

Whenever possible rock belays should be sought for as they are far superior to any snow or ice belay. However, this is not always possible and other methods have to be employed.

Belaying on Snow

1. Deadman (fig.1 page 87).

The most effective belay on snow is the deadman. This consists of a flat alloy plate about one foot square with a four foot wire sling attached to its centre. A "T" shaped slot is cut in the snow slope with care being taken not to disturb the snow on the down slope side. The plate is then inserted at an angle of about 40 degrees to the snow slope. This angle is obtained by placing an ice axe perpendicular to the slope and bisecting the angle between the shaft and the slope with the deadman; cast the deadman plate back a few degrees from this. Attach another sling to the wire sling to give a length of at least 6 feet and pull it tight in the centre slot. The sling should exit at the end of the slot. Check the depth of the deadman, using the ice axe to measure the distance from the wire attachment point to the surface of the snow. Cut a stance below the sling and belay in the normal way. Check that the deadman is "seated" by pulling tight on the belay. Avoid placing the deadman between two snow layers of different harness.

BELAYING ON SNOW

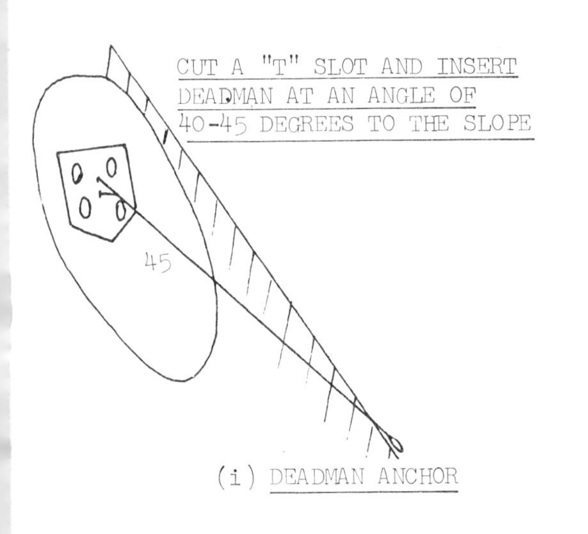

(i) DEADMAN ANCHOR

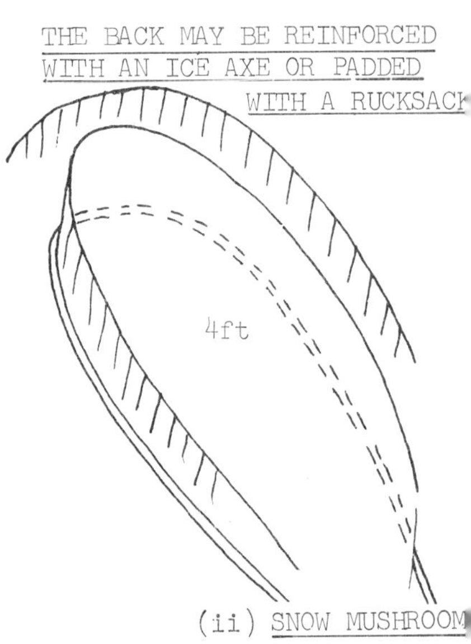

(ii) SNOW MUSHROOM

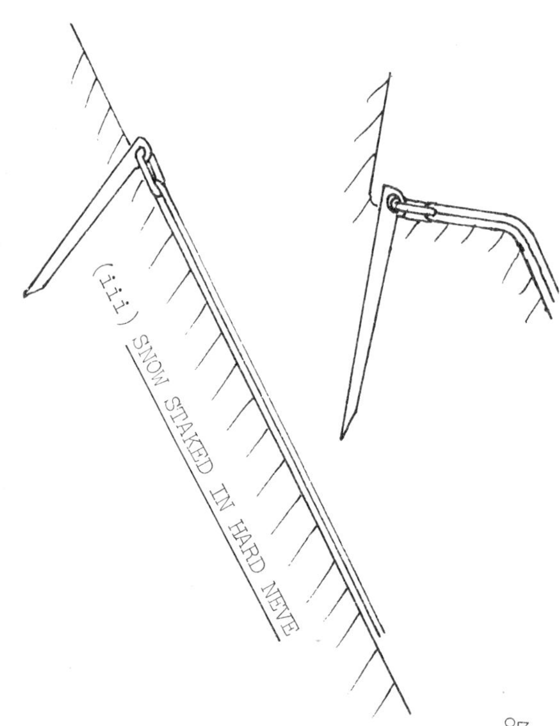
(iii) SNOW STAKED IN HARD NEVE

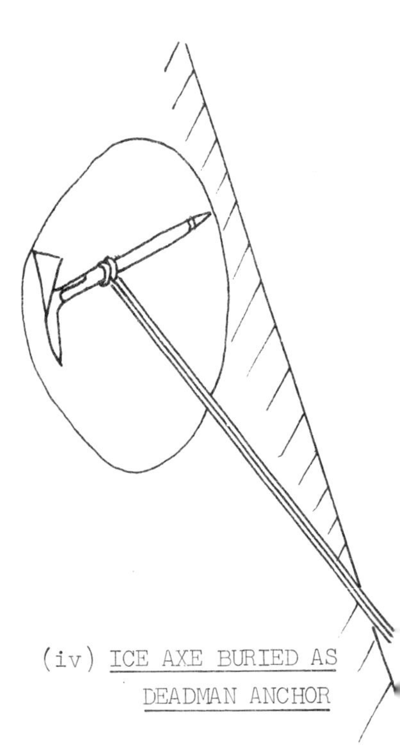
(iv) ICE AXE BURIED AS DEADMAN ANCHOR

In the absence of a deadman a sling may be clove hitched round the shaft of a strong ice axe shaft and the axe buried in he horizontal position in a T shaped slot. A shovel, ski, or piece f board may also be used. (Fig.4. Page 87).

2. Snow Mushroom (fig.2 page 87).

Another quite effective belay in hard snow is a snow mush-oom. This is a bollard cut out of snow with the size depending n the hardness of the snow - 3 or 4 feet across is usually ufficient. The climbing rope is then passed around the back of he bollard and the normal belay taken well below. The trench hould be at least a foot deep and the snow in front should be eft undisturbed. The anchor may be strengthened by placing ice xes at the back or by padding the rope around the bollard with ucksacks, spare clothes, newspapers, etc.

3. Ice Axe and Snow Stake Belays (fig.3-Page 87)

The ice axe and snow stake belays are really suspect and hould only be used in iron hard snow when time is pressisng. lace it at right angles to the slope and tilt the top back a few egrees from the vertical, then hammer home. (If there are spare eople available they can stand on the axe head and linked axe elays can be constructed one above the other.) Attach a long ling and belay well below this in a sitting position to ensure hat the belay rope runs almost parallel to the surface of the now. Another method of ice axe belay is to cut a large step and ammer the axe in vertically at the back of the step. This is also ore effective with a person standing on the axe head. Always use metal or fibre glass shafted axe for this method of belaying and nly use in iron hard snow.

Belaying on Ice

As with snow it is impossible to guarantee really secure belays on ice, however, in emergency they may have to be used.

1. Ice Bollard

In spite of the advances in ice screw design this is still probably the best belay on ice. A bollard is cut out of a solid boss of ice about 18 inches across and 24 inches long. The trench should be 6 inches deep and cut in at the back to hold the rope in position. Any starring or opaqueness in the centre of the bollar is an indication that it is unsound. (Fig.2. page 90).

2. Natural Anchors

Occasionally, natural ice anchors occur - ice pillars, natura ice pinnacles, edges and flakes of ice which can be cut into ancho points with the ice axe.

3. Ice Screws

There are three basic types of ice pitons. i.The drive in cut out old conventional type, which may now be regarded as obsolete. ii. The drive-in screw-release, and iii. The screw-in screw release. There is no ice screw or piton which is the ideal - the each have their advantages and disadvantages and one must use different screws for different types of ice. The Salewa tubular ice screw is suitable for brittle ice as it is hollow and extracts a core of ice as it is screwed in. The Salewa drive-in screw-release ice piton is good for other types of ice although it requires a great deal of effort to hammer into hard ice. The effectiveness of any type of ice screw ultimately depends upon the strength of the ice.

BELAYING ON ICE

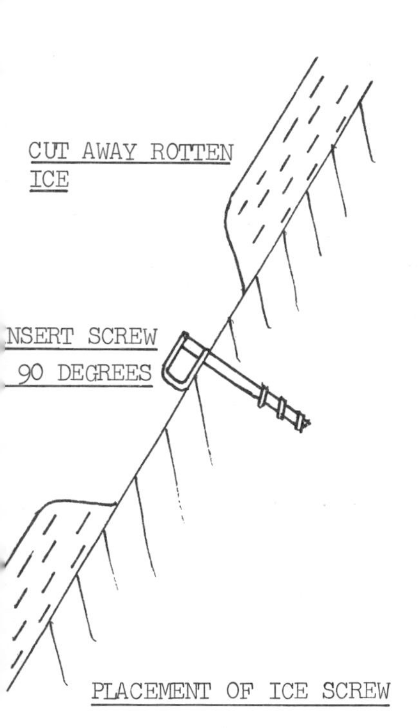

PLACEMENT OF ICE SCREW

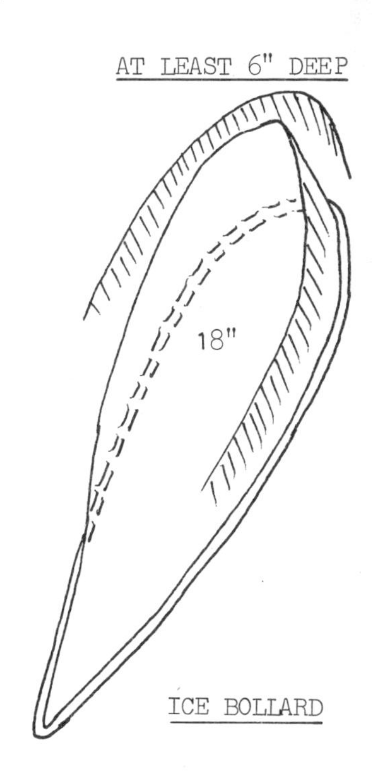

ICE BOLLARD

DINNER PLATING

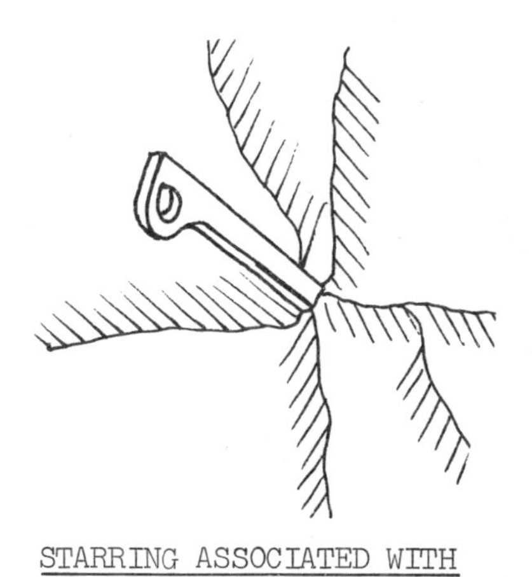
STARRING ASSOCIATED WITH OPAQUENESS IN THE ICE

Placement of Ice Screws (Page 90)

1. Always put into sound ice; if the surface is brittle or soft cut it away to expose the good ice below. As with a rock peg the head of an ice screw may afford support and it should be inserted with the eye down and the head flush to the ice. When cutting away rotten ice, to insert a drive-in screw-release piton, ensure there is sufficient clearance for the head to rotate for extraction.

2. The angle of insertion is 90 degrees.

3. Starring occurs in brittle ice with most screws although the Salewa tubular is less liable to cause starring than any others.

4. Dinner Plating - This occurs in brittle ice when the insertion of a piton chisels off large lumps of ice shaped rather like a dinner plate. Care should be taken when inserting an ice piton above head height, as the ice may break away onto the climber.

5. General - Always use more than one ice piton for a belay and link in the same way as rock pegs. Never place them too close together and always try to place them in separate ice bosses. Avoid placing an ice piton near the edge of a horizontal step as it may break off the lip of the step. A large step may be cut in easy angled ice and the piton placed near the back of the step in a vertical plane.

Notes On the Placement of Different Screws

1. Stubai corkscrew - cut a small hole with the pick of the axe to start the screw off.

2. Salewa tubular - cut a small hole with the pick of the axe to start the screw. Hammer slightly to start screw whilst screwing it at the same time. Use the pick or shaft of the axe or another screw as a lever in the karabiner eye hole.

ICE SCREW PLACEMENT

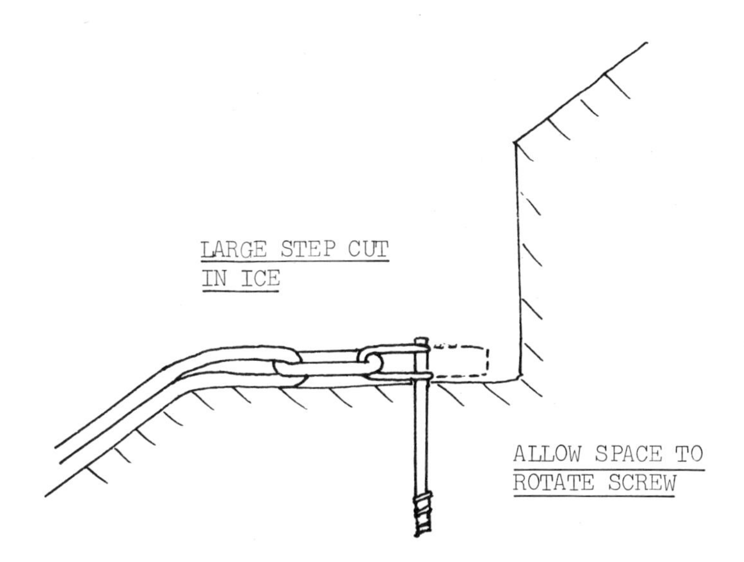

Linking Belays

In rescue situations secure belays are essential and it is sound policy to link belays for safety. All belays should be linked in such a way that the strain acts simultaneously on all the anchor points. In some instances it may be thought necessary to link all main belays with a rope, so each separate system backs up its neighbour. In the diagram (i) position (c) is supported by (a) and (b) and the connection ropes are tensioned so as to give immediate support. The adjusting of slings can be achieved by tying them in sheet bends which are easily adjustable, or by taking a twist of the spare rope around the karabiner. In diagram (iix) the failure of peg (b) will result in a swing and the shock loading of piton (a) which could then fail. The correct way to link pegs (a) and (b) would be to use two slings meeting midway and well below the pitons. Diagram (iii) shows an incorrect way of linking the pegs with separate slings. Again, if either peg fails, the sling will slide through the other and it will be shock loaded with a risk of failure.

All linking of pitons should take into consideration the type of placement of the piton and the direction of pull resulting from the linkage.

LINKING BELAYS

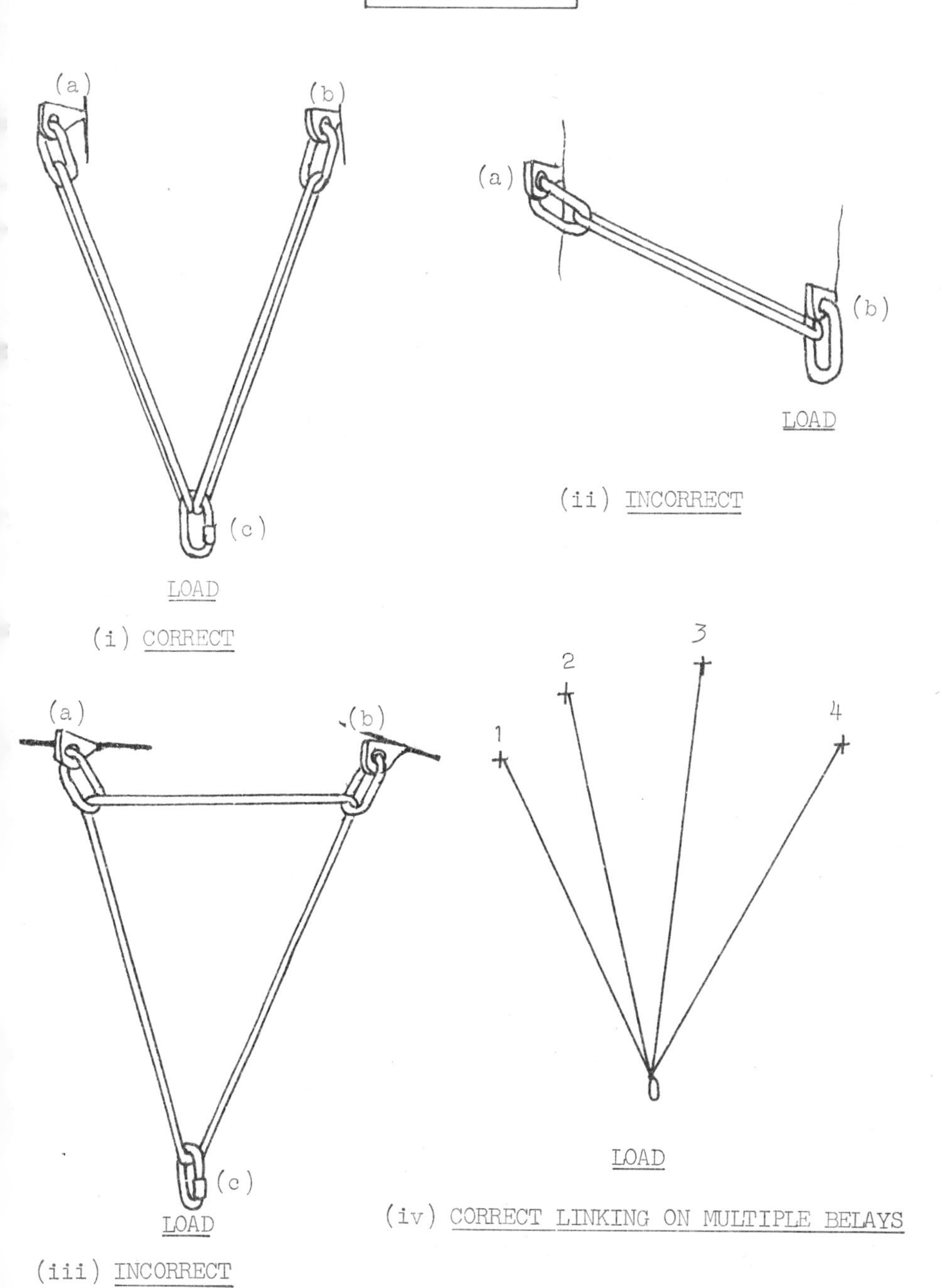